Part-Time
Work

PART~TIME WORK

Second Edition

Judith Humphries

Kogan Page

First published 1983 by Kogan Page Limited
120 Pentonville Road, London N1 9JN
Second edition 1986

British Library Cataloguing in Publication Data
    Humphries, Judith
    Part-time work. — 2nd ed.
    1. Part-time employment — Great Britain
    I. Title
    331.25'7   HD5110.2.G7

    ISBN 1-85091-139-8

Printed and bound in Great Britain by
Billing & Sons Limited, Worcester

Contents

Acknowledgements

The subject of this book is so wide that I should not have been able to write it without the help of many people. I should like to thank the *Guardian* newspaper, Her Majesty's Stationery Office, the Lothian Health Board and the Low Pay Unit for permission to print material. I am also indebted to the staff of Part Time Careers Ltd and particularly to the 32 part-time workers who spoke so freely to me of their experiences. Finally, I should like to thank Loulou Brown who edited the original script and Helen Steadman who undertook the arduous task of updating it for the second edition.

Judith Humphries
May 1986

Part 1

Introduction

The future of work is an issue fraught with concern. In the three years that have elapsed since the first edition of this book was written, unemployment has continued to rise and 'high tech' procedures have changed the nature of much of the work available. The future holds so much uncertainty that many people believe a radical restructuring of working patterns is needed. In contrast with this general picture, however, part-time work is still on the increase, yet with little qualitative difference. It has remained largely untouched by technological advances and the opportunities and issues of 1983 still hold good. For these reasons, the central theme of this book retains its relevance, concerned as it is with what it means to be a part-time worker.

Becoming a part-time worker means much more than increasing your free time and decreasing your wage, because part-time work is not like full-time employment. Even if you do the same type of work that you once did full-time you will be doing it under a different set of terms and conditions, so that in many instances you cannot be said to be doing the same job.

The structure of part-time work is complex — from finding a job in the first place to obtaining a retirement pension at the end of it. It can take a long time to sort out your position with regard to rights and benefits, and even longer to identify ways in which they might be extended. Most full-time employees are subject to the same provisions under employment law, but this is not the case with part-timers. Legally, the position is much more complicated, with a staggered system of benefits for which some workers qualify and others do not.

In the main, benefits are restricted if you are considered to be working part-time, so the question of definition is an important one. Employers usually regard all employees who work less than the standard number of hours in their workplace as part-timers, regardless of comparisons with other jobs. This means that a shop assistant employed for 35 hours a week or a junior hospital doctor working 40 or 50 hours a week will both be regarded as part-timers, although they work more hours than a full-time school teacher.

The Department of Employment considers all those who work for less than 30 hours to be part-timers, whereas employment law treats all employees who work for 16 hours or more a week on a par with full-timers. Hours worked can affect eligibility for some State benefits, and, in these cases, the benefits available to those assumed to be full-time workers are more favourable. There is thus no single definition of a part-time worker, but a multiplicity of regulations which all tend to treat those who work for fewer hours less favourably than those who work for more.

Part-time workers have traditionally been regarded as a marginal workforce, on tap when needed and otherwise dispensable, allowing a convenient flexibility in the workforce situation. Two factors have been largely responsible for this attitude. The first is that women have always formed by far the greater portion of the part-time workforce and the second is the assumption that people who work for fewer hours have a lesser commitment to their jobs.

The reality is that most part-timers are unable to work in any other way because they cannot. For example, they may be mothers with young children. Their 'choice' of fewer hours paid work is not made because they think a little work outside the home might be 'interesting', but is the result of their need to cope with home commitments — which cost money. There is no need to argue about the value of work. The work ethic is deeply embedded in British society, and, when they are given the opportunity, women show that they subscribe to it as much as men do. Yet women as employed people have less power and influence than men, and this lack of power is reflected very strongly in the structure of part-time work.

In quantitative terms, part-time work is on the increase. More people are employed part-time today than was the case a few years ago, despite the dramatic increase in unemployment in the total workforce. However, there has been little improvement in the type and conditions of part-time work, and this is a matter of grave concern. The need that many people have to work part-time, at least for a while, has been clearly demonstrated, and the problems relating to part-timing can no longer be shelved. With the employment situation in a state of crisis, and a growing number of people forcibly idle, or channelled into part-time work as their only employment option, it makes no sense to discriminate against part-time work. Suitable part-time work should be available on decent terms for all those who need or prefer it. At the moment there are many people occupying full-time posts who would prefer to work part-time but cannot either because comparable part-time jobs are unavailable, or because they are too restrictive.

It would be a pious hope, however, to expect help to come from outside however much this might make sense in general terms. Action to change the present situation must come from part-timers themselves. In formulating action it is vital that they have access to all the relevant information.

This book sets out to provide a comprehensive introduction to the nature of part-time employment, first setting it in an historical context and subsequently making suggestions for future reform.

Part 1 is devoted to facts which affect all part-timers: part-time employment patterns across the total occupational spectrum; employment legislation and the benefits structure; different modes of employment factors which influence the day-to-day quality of part-time work; and the effects of part-timing on ultimate career goals.

It is hoped that the information contained in this book will prove helpful to the reader in deciding and arranging his or her patterns of work, and that it will also contribute to the creation of a more informed workforce. Information is essential, because it is the best source of protection and the basis for reform.

Chapter 1

Who Works Part-time, When and Where?

Introduction

In September 1985 there were 20,882,500 people in employment. 9,340,000 were women, of whom 4,339,500 were part-time workers. Although the total number of employees in employment has rapidly declined in the 1980s, there has been a sharp increase in female part-time workers, from 3,781,000 in 1981 to 4,339,500 in 1985.*

It would be misleading, however, to assume from this that there is a general flowering of part-time opportunities in all types of jobs. Part-time work has always been concentrated in only a few occupations and the recent increase in the number of part-time jobs is almost entirely confined to this narrow field. The situation is mainly attributable to the predominance of women working part-time. Part-time work has been, both in theory and in practice, so much the province of women that patterns of female employment have dictated its structure.

Occupational Differences Between Male and Female Full-time Workers

There has always been a difference between the occupational grouping of men and women; though many barriers have been crossed, the differences still remain. The two main factors influencing this situation are differences in education and sex stereotyping, which confines many women to jobs which are extensions of their domestic role and preserves certain occupations exclusively for men.

Attitudes to education are at the root of occupational differences, as educational attainments pave the way to future work. They affect women in two ways: first, in the amount of education they receive and secondly in the form it takes. Thirty years ago, when women were expected to spend their lives in

* At the time of revision (April 1986) results of the 1984 Census of Employment were not yet available. Statistics have, instead, been taken from the *Employment Gazette* (March/April 1986) which only gives figures for women part-timers.

domesticity, the education of daughters was a matter of minor importance. The rich could go to finishing schools to acquire a few social graces and the poor had few educational opportunities even if they wanted them. They would work and 'get by' as their mothers had done before them. The majority in between were served up a diluted form of the education offered to boys, laced with such female pursuits as cookery and needlework, and most opted out of the educational system as soon as they could.

Despite the expansion of secondary and higher education since those days, the increase in female employment has not been equalled by an increase in the educational attainment of girls. Although girls do rather better than boys in tests at the age of 11, and equal them in the number of examination passes at 16, once they reach school leaving age they tend to discontinue their education in far larger numbers. Consequently, more girls than boys begin their first job with no higher qualifications or vocational training and this limits them in the kind of work they are able to do.

Girls who prolong their education tend to place themselves at another disadvantage through the choice of subjects they study. At secondary school, girls commonly reject maths, sciences and technological studies in favour of the humanities and such 'female' subjects as home economics. (In 1984, of girls and boys achieving at least one A level pass, 29 per cent of boys, but only 12 per cent of girls specialised in science and maths.) The demands of our increasingly technological society, which make sciences and technology safer recommendations for employment than the humanities, have prompted various investigations into why girls shun these subjects. The findings so far suggest that sciences and technology are seen to be 'unfeminine', and, therefore, socially disadvantageous. Hypotheses that girls are naturally better equipped to work descriptively, rather than logically and scientifically, are hard to substantiate because of the difficulty of separating innate tendencies from the influences of social conditioning.

Although almost as many young women as young men now go to universities, women tend to study humanities, education and social sciences — subjects which do not provide many job opportunities. On the other hand, few young women study subjects such as engineering, technology, forestry or agriculture, which are comparatively more vocationally oriented courses. (In

1984, fewer than one in ten university graduates in engineering and technology were women.)

Below degree level, polytechnics and colleges of further education offer many courses with a technical or technological bias. Despite the range of courses available, women usually restrict themselves to those offering secretarial and clerical skills. Other forms of training taken by women are those leading to nursing and childcare qualifications, which are only rarely taken by men.

Apprenticeship schemes offering training through day-release sessions provide many men with training for a variety of craft skills, but they attract very few women and only then in the more acceptable female activities such as horticulture. A female apprentice plumber or bricklayer still merits a half-page story in any newspaper. It is difficult to decide where the responsibility for this situation lies, but the facts remain: in 1984, of young people released by their employers for training at further education colleges, 70.8 per cent were male and 29.2 per cent female.

As a result of these educational patterns, and the more general ideas about what is suitable work for women which they reflect, full-time women workers are bunched in only a few occupational groups: education and health care, office work, retail distribution, and some light manufacturing industries, particularly in the food and clothing trades. Full-time male employment, on the other hand, is evenly distributed throughout all occupations, except that it is notably low in a few jobs which have traditionally been seen as 'women's work' such as nursing (except of mental patients), sewing, typing and food manufacturing.

The Occupational Structure of Part-time Work

Throughout the past 30 years, the time during which female employment generally has been steadily increasing, there has been a corresponding expansion of female part-time employment. In 1950, 11.8 per cent of women in manufacturing industries worked part-time and this had risen to 18.7 per cent by 1971. Between the censuses of 1966 and 1971, 403,000 more women entered part-time employment, and there was an even greater increase during the early 1970s, with the expansion of work opportunities in the service sector. When the recession set in in the mid-1970s there was a levelling off, but recently part-time work has been on the increase again. Today, 40 per cent of all women at work are part-timers. Male part-timing, on the other hand, has until recently been very restricted, and has rarely been the subject of statistical analysis.

Patterns of part-time work can be said to stem from the structure of full-time female employment, as most part-time work is found in those jobs which are either considered to be 'women's work' or are equally menial male equivalents of it. In hospitals, for instance, part-time women scrub the floors and part-time men do the portering and heavier domestic duties. There is a similar division of work tasks in shop work, which is another common source of part-time work.

Both the examples cited above are taken from work in the 'service industries', which is a term used to describe work (usually of a fairly humble nature) which provides a direct service to the public in the form of selling, cleaning and catering. Such work is a significant component of full-time female employment too, but in part-time employment a different balance is found. Whereas full-time women workers are fairly evenly represented in all the 'female' occupations, part-timers are concentrated in jobs in the service sector (85 per cent in 1978 — the most up-to-date statistics at the time of going to press) and correspondingly fewer women find employment in other fields.

Within the service industries, most part-timers work in two settings. The first is retail distribution where, according to the statistics in the *Employment Gazette* (March/April 1986), more women work part-time than full-time. The second has been described as 'other personal services' (*Women's Working Lives*, by Peter Elias and Brian Main, 1982) and comprises a variety of low-level cleaning and catering jobs mainly in the public sector. Most of the increase in the number of part-time workers is due to the expansion in numbers of jobs of this sort, and the evidence suggests that they are available to the exclusion of other kinds of work. A recent TUC report, ('Women in the Labour Market', 1983) reveals that one in 25 women doing low-skilled cleaning and catering work has a teaching qualification, one in 12 a nursing qualification, and one in six clerical and commercial qualifications. This information is particularly depressing in view of the fact that teaching, nursing and office work are among the more readily available occupations for suitably qualified full-time women.

In the manufacturing industries, part-time work patterns

17

roughly approximate to full-time female employment structure, with a concentration of opportunities in work involving monotonous light assembly work and continuous processes which benefit from the continuity provided by successive part-time shifts. Part-time work is present, to a lesser degree, in other occupations undertaken by full-time women workers, but almost never in the heavily male-dominated work areas. These restrictions apply to both male and female part-time workers, although there are very few men who work part-time in the manufacturing industries.

Overall, in comparison with female full-time workers, part-timers can expect a further restriction of opportunities, and a channelling of workers into unskilled manual jobs. The nature of these jobs, which can differ considerably from one workplace to another, will be discussed in Part 2 of this book, together with the situation found by those whose jobs demand the qualifications and training they may possess.

Reasons for Creating Part-time Jobs

Very little research has been carried out into the reasons for the creation of part-time jobs, and this makes the formulation of constructive policies for expanding part-time opportunities extremely difficult. Employees who wish to press for part-time posts they need must do so in a random fashion, and employers are given no incentive to widen their conception of the potential usefulness of part-time workers. As things stand, these conceptions are limited and it appears that part-time jobs arise for three main reasons: when the work to be done is more conveniently undertaken on a part-time basis; when a shortage of full-time labour causes employers to seek alternative sources; and when equipment or machinery is more effectively used by employing part-time shift workers.

The first reason arises when the work to be done does not occupy the full working day or week. It is commonly the case in cleaning and catering jobs, with school crossings patrols, and a whole range of occupations supporting the care of children in schools, parks, playgrounds and youth clubs. Part-timers are also employed for convenience, to provide back-up for the full-time staff at periods of peak activity. This need is felt in establishments dealing directly with the public, particularly shops and building societies.

At the present time, when there is high unemployment,

labour shortages are to be expected usually only in very specific circumstances. They arise when there are jobs which are too menial and low-paid to attract the (mainly male) full-timers, and where the greater part of the workforce is female and therefore liable to be lost when women leave to have children. Examples of the former are routine assembly work in light manufacturing industries (notably toy-making) and typical of the latter are office work and nursing. In such situations, employers often arrange part-time shifts to attract women back to work after they have had children.

The third reason for part-time jobs stems from manufacturing processes involving machinery which is more profitable the longer it is kept in operation. Some firms employ an evening shift to take over after the full-time day workers leave, in order to squeeze more productivity out of their equipment. This is only done in light manufacturing when the evening workforce is expected to be mainly female, and therefore assumed to be incapable of heavy work. Other firms, whose production involves continuous processes, may also organise day-time work on a part-time basis. This means that one shift can take over immediately from another, and machinery does not have to be shut down during lunch breaks. Examples include biscuit-making, confectionery and the tobacco trade.

There is also a rather different situation whereby part-time working is determined by the worker rather than by the employer. This situation occurs in types of manufacturing which can be carried on outside the factory, thus saving the employer the expense of accommodating certain workers on the premises. Such workers are known as homeworkers. Garment making is typical of the jobs done by homeworkers, who are allowed to decide on the amount of work they wish to do and can thus regulate their hours of work.

Apart from a very few exceptions — which involve enlightened employer attitudes, or needs specific to a particular job or profession — these appear to be the criteria for creating part-time work. It can be seen that they apply to a very limited range of occupations, of which a large proportion are very menial. Coupled with the fact that part-timers, across the board, enjoy few of the benefits of employment (see Chapter 2), it appears that employers exploit part-timers, and that their ability to do so is surely a major reason for employing them. There might, however, be another reason for the present job structure, which has to do with the education and qualifications of the part-timers themselves.

Who Works Part-time?

Most part-timers at the present time are older people, who received their education in the days when manual labour was the main source of work. For this reason, it is possible that the low-status jobs usually offered to them may, to some extent, reflect their own lack of skills and training. Today, there is a trend away from manual work towards technological skills and a demand for higher qualifications. When the people who are being educated in response to this reach the part-time labour market, they may modify it by their abilities and expectations. Until then, there is little prospect that the situation will change.

Very little is known of men who work part-time except that most of them are free of family responsibilities, being in the later stages of their working lives or, occasionally, at the very beginning. They, like women, are limited in the range of jobs open to them and they also suffer from disadvantages which women do not experience.

It is not generally accepted that an able-bodied man should want to work part-time. He is looked upon as odd, or a failure, by a society which measures success in terms of job-status, and which reckons men should be full-time breadwinners. It seems possible that a man might be regarded with suspicion when applying for a job which the employer had assumed would be taken by a woman. Unlike a woman, he will also be conditioned to expect (and will be expected by others to earn) a full-time wage. So men have to cope with attitudes which may well prevent them from seeking part-time work in the first place.

It is impossible to guess how many men would like to work part-time, had they the courage and opportunity. Many have already voiced their discontent at being absent so much from the life of their families, or having so little time to devote to other interests. Yet few avoid their 'enslavement' to full-time hours, especially during their middle years when there are the greatest pressures to 'get on' at work.

Women part-timers, on the other hand, are usually women with family commitments. More is known about them. One of the most recent studies, based upon the National Training Survey of 1975-6 (Elias and Main, 1982), attempted to establish patterns of part-time employment through tracing the work histories of individuals. It found that most part-timers were aged over 30, and were 'returners' to work after a period of several years away from employment. The consistency with which this pattern of a gap in employment emerged among women of all age groups, modified only by the tendency of younger women to spend less time out of employment than their seniors, led the authors to conclude that there is an overwhelming connection between female part-time working and childbearing. The study found that most part-timers are mothers with young children, and this fact surely acts as a further limitation to their choice of work because it influences the hours and the location at which they are able to work. It must also be a major influence on their whole working lives, as it means that women are least active in employment during the very years when men are most involved in consolidating their careers.

Hours of Work

When considering hours of work, part-timers probably fall into three groups: those with school age children who need a shortened working day; those with younger children who are only free to work when their partners are at home to take over child-care; and those who need more free time than the full working week affords but who are not tied to a regular routine. Jobs can be found that fit in with all these requirements, but the most plentiful involve working unsocial hours.

Many jobs in the service industries are secondary to the main occupation of a workplace, and are therefore most conveniently carried out outside normal working hours, that is, early in the morning or in the evening. Cleaning and supermarket shelf-filling are good examples of this type of work. Peak period working hours are unsocial too, as they occupy lunch times, late night opening and weekends. Most catering (except in schools), is geared to the times when people eat, rather than to the hours at which they expect to be at work. Then, too, there are the evening shifts in the manufacturing industries.

Part-time evening work is also carried out by professionals. Teachers take evening classes because there is surprisingly little part-time work available in day-time teaching; part-time youth workers are employed during evenings when the need is greatest; and part-time nurses tend to get the unpopular shifts. All this can be an advantage initially, when children are very young, but it can become a burden in future years if it proves to be a situation from which there is no escape.

Location of Work

Most part-timers work close to home, and some carry on their work in their own homes. Time is a precious commodity for the part-timer and too much travelling encroaches on the time limits available. It also adds to the expenses which must be met out of a relatively low wage packet. So most people, after they have decided how many hours they can work, have to identify the kinds of jobs which are available locally.

In some areas, the presence of manufacturing industries offering part-time shifts or homeworking will have forged patterns of part-time work, and young mothers may automatically follow their neighbours to the factory or take in homework. But jobs in the manufacturing industries are on the decline and many people will not have these opportunities in the future.

All areas, however, apart from the most rural, have local institutions in the public sector which are a major source of part-time work. Women part-timers are found in large numbers working in schools, other educational establishments, hospitals, and local councils. A few may be employed as teachers, nurses, doctors, or office workers, but the great majority will be engaged in domestic work of one sort or another — minding children, cooking meals, cleaning and helping the elderly in their homes. There is a fair degree of acknowledgement among public employers of the needs of working mothers, and work shifts often fit in with family life. Recently, there has also been a commitment on the part of local government to the idea of job-sharing (see Chapter 3, p 58), which is designed to open up part-time work in occupations which, traditionally, have been reserved for full-timers, so it is possible that in the future a broader range of jobs may be available in the public sector.

Outside the public sector, substantial numbers of shop workers and clerical workers in banking and insurance are employed part-time, so the well-known names in any local High Street are possible sources of work. In catering, there is a high proportion of part-timers, but it is as well to remember that a lot of such work involves extremely unsocial hours.

All the occupations mentioned above are open to men, but they rarely participate in them. Often, male part-timers are allotted different tasks within the same kinds of establishment. They may be employed as warehouse hands in retail distribution, as car park attendants, or on heavy packaging and porterage duties. There is one area of part-time work, however, where there are more men than women workers. This is agricultural work (see Chapter 7, p 128) in which, according to the 1981 Census of Employment, 31,000 men are employed part-time as against 30,000 women.*

Matching Jobs to Workers

The nature of the relationship between the jobs available and the abilities and skills of the potential workforce is shrouded in mystery, as are the numbers of people seeking part-time work. There are exact statistics of the numbers of full-time workers who are unemployed and this *should* be an important determinant in forming policies for creating more jobs. No comparable statistics are available for part-timers, however. This is because many part-timers are not eligible for unemployment benefit, and, as they gain no advantage from registering with an employment office, they tend not to do so.

If unemployed part-timers cannot be counted, it is difficult to imagine that they will be of any account in job-creation schemes. Many will slide out of the labour market without being regarded as unemployed. Many more, desperate for a wage of any kind, will take low level jobs for which they are unsuited. Outside the three-yearly Census of Employment, there is no machinery at present for monitoring this situation, and it is left to the part-timers themselves to raise their voices, and (perhaps) to the more scrupulous employers to publicise the number and the type of part-timers whose employment they have been forced to terminate.

Part-timers must use their initiative to find work from the limited opportunities available. Many part-time jobs are not advertised publicly, and appointments are often made as the result of personal inquiry, or on the recommendation of a friend. It is often left to the prospective employee to do the round of likely workplaces, and hope that at least one visit coincides with a vacancy. Some jobs are advertised in local papers or on postcards in the windows of corner shops, and

---

* Later figures of male part-time employment were not available at the time of writing.

some find their way to Jobcentres which keep separate information boards for part-time work.

The professions in the public sector usually advertise posts in their professional journals, but this is helpful only to people already on the inside who have access to such journals. There is no doubt that part-timers are at a disadvantage in their search for work if they have lost touch with their previous full-time employment. Many part-timers who manage to return to their original line of work do so by having maintained links with their once full-time employer.

Conclusion

To sum up, it must be stressed that part-time work is easy to come by only in certain occupations. As most part-timers are also ruled by the hours at which they can work, and the need to work close to home, the opportunities open to them are very restricted indeed. Most are part-timers of necessity rather than choice, and, to this extent, they are a captive workforce, on hand to fill gaps in the labour market at the employers' convenience. Not all part-timers are drudges, however. Many value and enjoy their work and jobs are not always what they might seem at first. There are hidden rewards in even the most menial jobs — and snags in those which appear ideal. Subsequent chapters will examine how this situation arises and will attempt an analysis of the circumstances which can combine to make a part-time job a satisfying experience.

Chapter 2

Legislation: Rights and Benefits for Part-time Workers

Introduction

All workers need some form of legal protection. They need to know that their jobs are secure and that they will work in a safe environment without unreasonable demands being made of them. They need to be assured that they will be free of arbitrary forms of discrimination, and that they will, if at all possible, have paid holidays and financial support at times of sickness, pregnancy or redundancy.

Protection of this nature comes from two sources: State benefits, administered by the Department of Health and Social Security (DHSS), and legally enforceable employment rights. Part-time workers are at a disadvantage on both counts, but they are somewhat more favourably treated by the DHSS than they are under employment legislation.

State benefits are those which are available to all workers, whether employed or unemployed. They include Unemployment and Supplementary Benefit, Family Income Supplement for low wage earners, sickness benefit, various grants such as maternity and death grants, and the State Retirement Pension. Most benefits are dependent on National Insurance contributions, but some, notably Family Income Supplement and Supplementary Benefit, are not. The State benefit scheme will be discussed later in this chapter (see pp 44-52) following an examination of those rights and benefits relating specifically to employment.

Employment Rights

Employment rights offer essential protection to workers. They include the right to work in a safe environment, without discrimination on grounds of race or sex, and they cover such aspects as job security and redundancy arrangements, unfair dismissal, statutory sick pay and maternity leave. They can also be extended to include rulings on paid holidays and other fringe benefits of employment. These rights do not, however, apply equally to all workers. Part-timers generally are less favourably treated than full-time workers and there is one category of workers (those who work less than eight hours a week) which is excluded altogether from employment rights.

To be eligible for employment rights as summarised above, you must be an *employee*, an applicant for employment or a trainee. The Employment Protection (Consolidation) Act 1978 (Section 153) defines an employee as one who has entered into or works under a contract of employment (see p 43). Section 146 excludes people in certain occupations, such as policemen and judges, who *hold office*, but do not have a contract of employment, though other forms of employment protection are usually open to them. Furthermore, a contract of employment, for the purposes of the Act, is one in which the employee works under a contract *of service*. This excludes many people who are defined as self-employed because they work under a contract *for services*.

Other criteria can be used to establish employee status. For example, if you are paid a *salary* rather than piecework rates or fees for items of work; if you can prove that you are under the control of an employer; if your work forms an integral part of an employer's business; if the facts of your case point to your standing in an employee relationship to an employer.

There are precedents for changing employment status from employee to self-employed and *vice versa* without changing the nature of the work or the nature of the essential arrangement between employer and worker. Such decisions, once made, will be upheld in law, even if they are subsequently challenged.

Despite the fact that these criteria exist for establishing employment status the complexity of the law prevents many people from securing their due rights. It enables many employers to deny employee status (and therefore to sidestep their obligations) to many workers from whose work they benefit. It is advantageous for an employer to designate workers as self-employed, because he or she thereby escapes from employment law responsibilities, and from the tax and National Insurance liabilities which employers must carry on behalf of employees. Custom and practice, therefore, have established certain categories of workers who are rarely regarded as employees. These include homeworkers, temporary and casual workers, freelancers, and the specifically self-employed.

Although many workers in these categories might be able to establish employee status in the courts, they are unlikely to be freely offered it. For this reason, work of these kinds may be assumed to carry a penalty: you will, almost certainly be self-employed, and for this reason you will not benefit from the provisions of employment protection legislation.

Employment rights are of three kinds: statutory rights conferred by Acts of Parliament; negotiated rights proceeding from agreements between employers and trade unions or other negotiating bodies; and rights granted by employers through their contracts of employment.

Statutory Rights
Statutory rights are the minimum rights for employees which all employers must observe. They are conferred by Acts of Parliament each of which covers different areas of interest. Readers wishing to check legislation at its source will find that there may be several Acts of a similar nature as important legislation is often reconsidered, added to, and partially amended. The most important Acts of Parliament which decide the statutory rights of employees are as follows: the Employment Protection Act 1975, the Employment Protection (Consolidation) Act 1978, the Employment Acts of 1980 and 1982, the Trade Union and Labour Relations Act 1974 (amended 1976), the Health and Safety at Work Act 1974, the Race Relations Act 1976, the Sex Discrimination Act 1975 and the Equal Pay Act 1970 (amended 1984). There are appeals procedures which employees can follow if they consider that their rights as defined under any one of these Acts have been infringed, and these will be outlined in the appropriate sections. Under the provisions of some of the above mentioned Acts the same rights are accorded to all employees. Under the provisions of others of these Acts, however, a sliding scale of eligibility for rights is established which tends to discriminate against part-timers.

ACTS GRANTING THE SAME PROTECTION TO ALL EMPLOYEES
Equal treatment for all employees, whether they work full-time or part-time, is established in matters relating to health and safety, discrimination on grounds of race or sex, and the right to protection from victimisation for lawful trade union activities. It should be noted, however, that disabled people are not protected from discrimination on account of their disablement. The Disabled Persons Employment Act 1944

which states that employers employing more than 20 workers should employ a fixed proportion of disabled people has never been properly implemented. Many disabled people are part-time workers.

The Trade Union and Labour Relations Act 1974 (amended 1976) gives trade unions and individuals extensive immunities when they commit civil wrongs in furtherance of industrial action. The extent of immunities has subsequently been reduced by the Employment Acts of 1980 and 1982. Protection for all employees from victimisation by their *employers* for trade union activities is codified in the Employment Protection Act (1978) as amended by the 1982 Employment Act (see p 33).

The Health and Safety at Work Act etc, 1974 applies to home-working. It requires all employers to ensure, so far as is reasonably practicable, the health, safety and welfare at work of all their employees. This includes those homeworkers in their employ. And it requires them to ensure, so far as is reasonably practicable, that persons not in their employment who may be affected by the conduct of their undertaking are not exposed to risks to their health and safety. This includes those self-employed homeworkers to whom they put out work. Health and safety regulations made under the Act apply to home-workers.

The Race Relations Act 1976 seeks to eliminate discrimination of all kinds on the grounds of racial origin. The employment provisions of the Act make it illegal for racial discrimination to be practised in matters of training, recruitment, employment and promotion and accord a measure of protection to non-employees.

The Sex Discrimination Act 1975 makes sex discrimination unlawful in employment, training and related matters, among other things. Employment only is discussed here. It defines various types of discrimination. Direct discrimination is the less favourable treatment of a person on the grounds of his or her sex in comparison with a person of the opposite sex; indirect discrimination involves practices which, although applied equally to both sexes, have a discriminatory effect, whether or not this is intended. The Act also defines as discrimination the victimisation of a person who has asserted his or her rights under the Act, or the Equal Pay Act (see p 29).

The coverage of the employment provisions of the Act includes discrimination by employers, employment agencies, certain vocational training bodies, trade unions, employers' associations and bodies granting licences or other qualifications which facilitate the carrying on of a particular trade or occupation. It therefore offers an extent of protection to all workers, regardless of whether they are employees.

The Act is to be amended under the Sex Discrimination Bill, published in February 1986. This is intended to remove restrictions on women's hours of work, which previously prevented them from taking manufacturing jobs based on shift or night work in factories and would make a number of changes to the Sex Discrimination Act, including narrowing the exemption for employment in private households and removing the exemption for employment with firms of five or fewer employees. The Bill also seeks to make it unlawful for a woman to be compelled by her employer to retire at an earlier age than a man would be in comparable circumstances.

The Equal Pay Act 1970 aims to eliminate discrimination in matters of pay, including overtime, piecework rates and holiday entitlements. The Act gives all employees the right to equal treatment with an employee of the opposite sex in the same employment who is doing the same, or 'broadly similar' work, or work rate equivalent under a job evaluation scheme, or work of equal value.

The effects of the Acts are as follows:

First, no employer may hound or dismiss you on account of your trade union activities, as long as these fall within the (restricted) provisions of the 1980 and 1982 Employment Acts. Many employers, however attempt (often with success) to oppose the setting up of union branches at their premises, as the Grunwick incident of 1977 so vividly demonstrated. The Employment Act 1980 has made their task easier by abolishing the procedure by which trade unions were able to enlist the help of the Advisory Conciliation and Arbitration Service (ACAS) in settling trade union recognition disputes.

Second, you are protected under the Race Relations Act 1976 and Sex Discrimination Act 1975 from racial or sexual discrimination in matters of recruitment, treatment, training and promotion, and from any form of victimisation on racial or sexual grounds. There are some limited exceptions to this, under the Sex Discrimination Act, for example, where sex is a genuine occupational qualification for a job, eg for reasons of authenticity, such as an acting job, or in order to preserve decency or privacy, such as in the case of a lavatory attendant. There are also certain exceptions to the non-discriminatory rulings of the Race Relations Act. For instance, if a person of a certain race is required to work in a helping capacity with a particular ethnic group. In such a case the job advertisement may stipulate a racial preference, but must state clearly the clause in the Act which makes an exception of the job appointment.

Third, if you are a woman doing the same work as a man, or if it is 'broadly similar' work, and you are both working for the same employer, you are entitled to the same rate of pay and other terms of employment as a man. You are also entitled to the same rate of pay if you are employed in a job which, though *different* from that of a man, has been given equal value under a proper 'job evaluation study'. And the third category of entitlement, introduced in 1984, allows claims for equal pay when the work is of equal value in terms of the demands made (for instance, in terms of effort, skill and decision making). However, a woman will have no claim under the equal value provisions if an 'analytical' job evaluation study has already rated her job as lower than a man's with whom she claims equal pay, unless she can show that the study is discriminatory on the grounds of sex.

Protection from discrimination on the grounds of sex is particularly important for part-time workers. First because they are often employed under less favourable terms and in lower status jobs than full-timers, and second because five out of six part-timers are women, and there is a tendency for women to be less favourably treated in employment across the board. Many of the differences in the treatment of part-time and full-time workers amount to sex discrimination and could be eliminated if the anti-discrimination laws were fully effective. Sadly this is not the case. Although immediately after the passing of the Equal Pay and Sex Discrimination Acts women's pay rose to 75 per cent of men's pay, by 1984 it had fallen back to 59 per cent of men's earnings in non-manual work and 61.5 per cent in manual work. However, it remains to be seen if the amendment of 1984 will substantially redress the balance. Present signs are encouraging: in April 1985, women's average hourly earnings (excluding overtime) were 74 per cent of men's (New Earnings Survey). Under present legislation, people may experience practical problems in deciding which Act applies in any one case, and some may find that their particular circumstances fall between the two.

APPEALS PROCEDURES
There is an established procedure for contesting the infringement of any of the above mentioned rights by bringing a case before an industrial tribunal. The procedure for doing so is weighted in favour of the employers and against the employee. Legal aid is not available, and cases can only be brought by individuals, not groups. It is also up to the individual claiming a grievance to prove it, and costs can be awarded against him or her if it is considered that a case has been brought unreasonably.

Union representatives will usually help or advise, but many part-timers work in small establishments with inadequate union representation or in non-unionised sectors of employment. In this case a solicitor can give advice, for a small fee, under what is known as the 'Green Form Scheme' or the 'Solicitors' Advice Scheme'. Solicitors participating in the schemes are listed in the Law Society's Referral List to be found in libraries and Citizens' Advice Bureaux (CABs).

In any event, it takes a lot of courage and conviction to bring a case on an individual basis, so it is possible that abuses of statutory rights go uncontested. This is particularly likely to be the case with part-time workers, who are often poorly paid and may feel isolated and less sure of their image as workers than their full-time colleagues.

Some progress in the right direction has been made through the influence of the EEC. Article 119 of the Treaty of Rome prohibits the payment of lower than full-time rates to part-timers who work in jobs which are wholly or predominantly done by female workers, unless this can be justified on grounds which do not constitute sex discrimination. Rulings on individual cases taken to the European Court of Justice have resulted in subsequently more favourable decisions by the British Employment Appeals Tribunal. The procedure for bringing a complaint continues to be both cumbersome and formidable, despite official denials.

The ineffectiveness of the procedure for enforcing the Acts so far described is borne out by the low rate of appeals brought under their provisions, and the even lower rate of complaints which are upheld in the courts. There was a steady decline in the number of cases brought under the Sex Discrimination

Act, from 243 in 1976 to 150 in 1982, although the position then improved somewhat, with 265 cases in 1983 and 310 in 1984. But of this last figure, 196 cases were settled or withdrawn, including a conciliated settlement before a tribunal hearing, and of the remaining 114 cases, 66 were dismissed by the tribunal.

Figures for cases brought under the Equal Pay Act 1970 show an even more drastic decline, yet inequalities in wages, especially for women part-timers, remain. In 1976, 1,742 cases were brought under the Act, but, by 1984, the number had reduced to a mere 70. Of this small number, 46 cases were withdrawn before a tribunal hearing and only 11 complaints out of the remaining 24 were upheld by the tribunal. Little is known of the reasons why people withdraw their cases, but it may be assumed that many are discouraged when they realise that circumstances militate against the individual who brings such a case.

In 1982 the European Court ruled that Britain was failing to fulfil its European obligations to ensure workers equal pay for work of equal value. This forced the Conservative Government to amend the Equal Pay Act, and the new amendments came into force in January 1984.

Since the 'equal value' amendments were introduced, there have been some encouraging signs. In 1984 and 1985 over 200 women made equal value claims. Many of these were settled out of court, but some were also successful at the tribunal: for instance, Julie Hayward, a shipyard canteen worker, who compared her job with that of skilled manual workers, and 15 Hull fishpackers, who compared their work with that of manual labourers.

It used to be difficult for part-timers to claim equal pay, as the industrial tribunals ruled that being a part-timer counted as a 'genuine material difference'. However, the position of part-time employees *vis-à-vis* the Equal Pay Act was ameliorated by the decision of the European Court of Justice in the case of *Jenkins v Kingsgate* (1981) ICR 592. The court ruled that 'a difference in pay between full-time and part-time workers does not constitute discrimination prohibited by Article 119 of the Treaty of Rome unless it is, in reality, merely an indirect way of reducing the pay of part-time workers who are wholly or predominantly women'. When the case was referred to the Employment Appeals Tribunal, a ruling was made that any variation in the pay of full- and part-time workers must be justified by reference to some object which is non-discriminatory on sexual grounds. As many groups of part-timers are 'wholly or predominantly women' it may now be more difficult for employers to justify paying them lower rates.

PROTECTION GRANTED TO EMPLOYEES ON A SLIDING SCALE

Employment Law — The main body of legislation affecting employees is determined by the Employment Protection Act 1975, the Employment Protection (Consolidation) Act 1978 and the Employment Acts of 1980 and 1982. The provisions of these Acts will be referred to as 'employment law'.

Legislation, introduced by the Labour Government between 1974 and 1979, had the effect of expanding the statutory rights of employees, including those of part-timers. The Employment Acts of 1980 and 1982 redressed the balance. Their main purpose is to curb the power of trade unions, but in the process they curtail the effective rights of individual workers in various ways.

Criteria for Assessing Eligibility for Statutory Rights — Statutory rights under employment law are granted to employees on the basis of the number of hours they work each week, the principle being that the more hours you work the more rights you get. These rights are not granted automatically, but are earned after a period of continuous employment with the same employer. The size of your workplace can also affect your eligibility for certain benefits. Employers of fewer than six workers are not obliged to grant their women workers the right to return to work after maternity leave. Many people are unaware of this legislation and, especially if they are combining work with family responsibilities, may take a new job for its convenience without realising that it can reduce their rights and benefits by breaking their continuity of employment, placing them with an employer who is exempt from certain obligations, or bringing them just below the requisite number of working hours.

Assessing Rights by Hours Worked and by Continuity of Employment — The easiest method of sorting through the legislation is by reference to the length of the working week and to the time spent in continuous employment. The Employment Protection Act 1975 extended the same basic rights to all employees working for 21 hours or more a week. In 1977, the required hours were reduced to 16 or more a week, and this remains a part of employment law. Stipulations were also made about the length of time an employee must be continuously employed to become eligible for each right. The rules for the computation of 'continuous employment' are among the most abstruse and complex in employment law (see Schedule 13 of the Employment Protection Act 1975). Continuous employment is defined as employment without *any* break with the same employer. There is a legal presumption of continuity and, once an employee can show the date on which employment began, this is presumed to be continuous until the employer proves to the contrary. An employee may change the place of work, the terms of employment, or even the contract of employment, without breaking continuity *if* he or she remains with the same employer.

Difficulties arise in dealing with the irregularities which occur in individual situations. There is a mass of legislation to deal with them, the main points of which are as follows:

- ☐ Breaks for holidays do not break continuity as long as the employee is under a contract which normally involves working that week.
- ☐ In cases of sickness or injury, the first 26 weeks of absence count towards continuity.
- ☐ If absence is caused through a temporary lay-off of workers (*not* by strike action taken by the employee) continuity is maintained. However, an employee loses continuity if absent through an interruption in the availability of work which he or she would otherwise perform. For instance, a part-time teacher employed on a seasonal basis loses continuity if the contract of employment is ended each July and renewed each September. This commonly happens.
- ☐ If an employee is absent by arrangement or custom (see p 57) continuity is maintained.
- ☐ If an employee goes on strike, continuity is broken.
- ☐ If there is a change of employer due to a take-over bid, the death of an employer or the transfer of business from one employer to another, continuity may be preserved.
- ☐ Employment may be continuous if the employee changes the place of work within associated companies.

The law becomes particularly complex for people whose hours of work change above and below 16 hours a week, as different provisions are made for employees in each of these categories.

The main legislation allows:

(a) That if an employee can show that for 26 weeks he or she worked for 16 hours or more a week *irrespective of the contracted hours*, these weeks count towards continuity. On the other hand, if the employer can prove that hours beyond those contracted were worked *voluntarily*, and the contracted hours fall below 16, continuity must be differently computed (see p 36).

(b) If an employee changes from 16 or more hours of work to between 8 and 16, he or she is attributed 26 weeks towards continuity.

Any week away from work for any other reason breaks continuity, although there *are* rules which allow for joining together separate periods of employment to establish continuity.

The rights are set out below. Note should be taken of the qualifying period, which is the length of time you must work continuously for the same employer to become eligible for a right.

Statutory rights of workers with employee status dependent on 16 plus hours worked a week

	Qualifying period of continuous employment
1. Time off for trade union duties and activities	No qualifying period
2. Unfair dismissal	One year qualifying period Two years qualifying period
3. Unfair dismissal for pregnancy	One year qualifying period*
4. Written reasons for dismissal	Six months qualifying period
5. Minimum period of notice	One month qualifying period

---

* In a recent case it was held that dismissal due to pregnancy can constitute unlawful sex discrimination, in which case no qualifying period of employment is necessary.

6. Written statement of contract (terms and conditions)	One month qualifying period
7. Maternity pay	Two years by the 11th week before confinement
8. Right to reinstatement after birth	Two years by the 11th week before confinement
9. Redundancy pay	Two years qualifying period
10. Time off to look for work	Two years qualifying period
11. Written statement of redundancy pay calculation	Two years qualifying period
12. Guarantee pay	One month qualifying period
13. Medical suspension pay	One month qualifying period
14. Itemised pay statement	First pay day

Those rights that are dependent on building up and maintaining continuous service are also extended to people who work between 8 and 16 hours a week, after they have worked continuously for the same employer for five years. This time qualification effectively excludes many part-timers from benefit, however, as it is unusual for five years' continuous employment to be achieved by people working these hours. For a start, considerable goodwill is required on the part of employers, who must retain the services of workers who have no job security in law. The personal circumstances of part-timers, too, militate against continuity of employment. Most people working for less than 16 hours are women with children, or other family responsibilities, and are probably not earning enough to be the sole wage-earner. Their jobs will be considered secondary to those of their husbands and, if their husbands move, they will move. If there is a crisis in the family — ill-health, or a problem with child-minders — the wife may be forced to give up her job to cope with it. It is no small undertaking for most people with such commitments considering part-time work to set out with the intention of clocking up the necessary five years' employment to earn their statutory rights.

Job Security — Probably the most essential of the statutory rights listed above is the right to protection from unfair dismissal. Many employers regard part-timers as the most expendable section of their labour force and will dispense with their services to suit their own convenience if they are legally able to do so. This makes part-time work an insecure form of employment for people working less than 16 hours a week.

So, the importance of working for at least 16 hours a week cannot be over-emphasised. If you work for 16 or more hours a week, you can achieve protection under employment law; if you work less than 16 hours a week you are unlikely to. If your hours fall below eight hours worked each week, you are barred from all but the most basic protection — that against racial and sex discrimination and victimisation for lawful trade union activities. This legislation discriminates against an alarming proportion of part-time workers.

Even if you work for 16 hours or more, it will be two years before you have job security and can take maternity leave or claim redundancy pay. It is the same for full-timers, too, but statistics show that part-timers are less likely to have a record of continuous employment. And if you work in an establishment which employs no more than five people, you may be unable to return to work after pregnancy, as your employer has no statutory obligation to take you back. There are hidden snags in the provisions of the Acts of Parliament outlined above — especially for part-timers.

Maternity Leave — The regulations concerning maternity leave have become more complex with the Employment Act 1982 and should be set out in some detail. *All* working women, whether part-time or full-time, are now permitted paid time off work to attend ante-natal clinics, as long as they produce evidence of their pregnancies and of medical appointments, and those who have been continuously employed for two years by the 11th week before the expected date of confinement may take maternity leave from that date, until 29 weeks after the week in which the baby is born. This is the maximum period permitted and there is no reason why you should stop work for so long unless you wish to do so. All women who take leave are entitled to maternity pay and to reinstatement in their jobs. This last right, however, has been eroded by the Employment Act 1980. It is now possible for an employer to offer 'suitable alternative' employment to a woman returning from maternity leave, but the Act does not clearly define what 'suitable alternative' may mean. It is therefore possible for employers to demote women returning after pregnancy, who have no means of redress. Furthermore, any employer employing fewer than six workers is exempted altogether from the obligation to allow women to return to work.

The procedure to be followed in taking maternity leave is outlined below:

1. 21 days before absence begins, the woman must inform the employer in writing:
   (a) that she will be leaving;
   (b) the date of the expected week of confinement;
   (c) that she intends to return to work.
2. Not earlier than 49 days after expected week of confinement:
   (a) the employer may make written request for confirmation of the woman's intention to return to work;
   (b) the woman must give written confirmation within 14 days of receiving request or as soon as reasonably practicable thereafter. The employer must advise the woman in writing that her failure to reply will mean that she loses her right to return to work.
3. The woman must give 21 days' written notice of proposed date of return.

Maternity leave is probably responsible for more prejudice against women workers than anything else. Many employers fear that, if they employ women, they will become heavily involved in maternity leave, but this is far from the case. A study, by the Policy Studies Institute, of women who had babies in February and March 1979 found that only about half of those who worked during their pregnancies qualified for maternity leave. With the odds stacked against part-timers, it is probable that most of these were full-time workers.

Another fear among employers who find themselves required to grant maternity leave is that the women involved will not repay them for their expense and inconvenience by continuing in their jobs. It is true that many women do not return to their jobs after taking leave, but the fault is not entirely theirs when State provision for childcare is minimal. Also, parenthood is an emotional business and no one can be sure how he or she will react to it until it happens. It seems reasonable for society as a whole to assume some responsibility for the birth and upbringing of future generations by providing facilities for continuing employment for those women who wish to use them.

Statutory Sick Pay — Since April 1983 employers have been responsible for paying sick pay to their employees. Until 5 April 1986 this responsibility only covered the first eight weeks of illness in a tax year. However, from 6 April 1986 changes in Social Security legislation remove the SSP link with tax years and increase the employers' responsibility for paying SSP to 28 weeks in one period of incapacity for work. Two periods of incapacity for work will link and be treated as the same if they occur within eight weeks of each other. If exceptionally a period of incapacity for work is still running three years after it started, liability for SSP will cease at the end of the third year. An important point to note is that someone whose average weekly earnings are lower than the National Insurance threshold (£38 a week from April 1986) will not have the right to SSP. It is therefore important — because payment of National Insurance contributions affects other benefits as well — that you try to earn enough to pay National Insurance contributions. Some employers pay more than the statutory minimum rates.

Appeals Procedures — Employees who consider that any one of their statutory employment rights has been infringed can appeal to an industrial tribunal (see p 31) and, if the appeal is successful, they will be awarded compensation and/or reinstatement. Since the passing of the Employment Act 1980, which was designed to help small businesses, it has become more difficult for employees to win appeals against unfair dismissal. The qualifying period for eligibility for this right was first increased from 26 weeks to one year, and since June 1985 has been extended to two years for all employees. Criteria for assessing the fairness of a dismissal now include consideration of 'the size and administrative resources of the employer's undertaking' and this has the effect of shifting the onus of proof, in relation to whether the employer acted reasonably, away from the employer and on to the employee. These new provisions hit part-timers, as many are employed in small businesses.

Similarly, a woman's right to bring a case for unfair dismissal after maternity leave has been reduced because employers may now offer 'suitable alternative' work. Whereas, in the past, an employer who was not willing to reinstate a woman in the *same* job had no recourse but to dismiss her, that same employer can now clothe the dismissal in the guise of 'suitable alternative' work. If the employee refuses this, *she* is considered to have terminated her contract of employment. She must also follow exactly the new complex procedure for taking maternity leave, or she will lose her right to return to work.

Negotiated Agreements
In addition to statutory rights, trade unions can negotiate with employers to obtain further rights and better conditions for their members at a particular workplace, and it is usual for them to do so. However, they have limited powers to negotiate on behalf of workers who are not employees. Negotiated agreements operate in two main ways: first, to improve on the statutory minimum (for instance, by obtaining more favourable terms of sick pay, maternity leave and redundancy pay for which employees who are excluded under State legislation may also be eligible) and second, to obtain concessions on matters which State legislation does not deal with. Paid holidays, leisure breaks, training and promotion arrangements, company pension and superannuation schemes, and, above all, wages and salaries, are matters which trade unions take up. Trade unions also help their members to exercise their legal rights.

Negotiated agreements, therefore, are important, both for filling the gaps in State legislation and for responding to the needs of a particular group of workers. Those who are the most disadvantaged in terms of rights and working conditions have most need of negotiated agreements — and this applies particularly to part-timers.

TRADE UNION ATTITUDES TO PART-TIME WORKERS
The extent to which any union will exert itself on behalf of part-time workers depends both upon the will within the union, from national down to branch level, and upon the strength of part-time membership. Traditionally, part-timers have been held under suspicion by many unions, as a potential threat to full-time jobs and as an exploited workforce which can undercut a union's bargaining power. Attitudes have been passive, or even hostile, and unions have been ready to agree that part-time workers are excluded from many negotiated benefits, and that, in times of recession, redundancies should hit part-timers first.

However, there are signs that attitudes are changing. Pressure from the TUC resulted in the extension of rights to all employees who work 16 hours or more a week. This became law in 1977, through an amendment to the Employment Protection Act 1975. At TUC Congress in 1980, a motion was passed demanding parity, *pro rata*, for part-timers, with full-time workers and a further motion, passed in 1986, called on the TUC to prepare a detailed report on the rights, pay and conditions of part-timers (see Appendix A).

Greater attention has also been paid to the position of women in trade unions. The TUC Charter, 'Equality for Women within Trade Unions', was published in 1979, and since then many trade unions have responded to women's demands for equal opportunities and increased involvement in union activities by recognising the need for childcare facilities at union meetings, training programmes for women managers, and the setting up of committees to promote equal rights within the unions. All these are moves in the right direction, and they have been matched at national level, if not in the branches, by individual unions. Many unions produce pamphlets aimed at part-timers and some have undertaken researches among their members. For instance, the National and Local Government Officers Association's (NALGO) 'Part Timers' leaflet reveals important facts about the position of women and part-time workers as a whole, and it is a step towards making proposals for future reform.

Some of the most notable efforts towards improvements for part-timers by trade unions have been made on behalf of homeworkers. Many homeworkers work part-time as non-employees in low status occupations. They are the least advantaged of all employment groups. The National Union of Hosiery and Knitwear Workers (NUHKW) and the General and Municipal Workers' Union (GMWU) have made attempts to unionise homeworkers, and have sponsored or have participated in campaigns to improve their working conditions and status.

Undoubtedly, however, part-time workers are under-represented in the trade union movement as a whole. Those who are likely to find most difficulty in joining a union, or indeed in finding a union to join, are homeworkers and those working in small, local businesses and factories. For people in this position, advice and information on trade unions may be forthcoming from community groups, women's groups, or other voluntary organisations. To find the addresses of these local organisations, ask at the Citizens' Advice Bureau or public library.

WAGES COUNCILS

If you are working in an industry where union representation is weak, or non-existent, the chances are that you are covered by a Wages Council. Wages Councils evolved from the 'Trade Boards', set up at the beginning of this century to protect workers in those industries where conditions were particularly bad, and today their main role is to undertake wage negotiations in occupations where the negotiating power of unions is insufficient. There is a separate Council for each industry, which sets a Statutory Minimum Rate (SMR) of pay for all workers within it. If you work in an industry covered by a Wages Council, particulars of rulings on pay rates should be displayed at your workplace, and your employer is liable to prosecution if he pays you less than the minimum rate. This applies to *all* workers, whether they work on the premises or at home, and it is a notable, but rare, example of a negotiated right which is extended to non-employees. Regrettably, many homeworkers are unaware that they have this protection.

The regulations are enforced by an inspectorate to whom complaints about wages abuses can be made. Unfortunately, the system has limited effectiveness. In 1983, nearly 40 per cent of establishments visited after complaints had been made were found to be underpaying their workers. There seem to be three reasons for this high failure rate. First, the Wages Councils' directives are so complex that many employers do not understand them; second, many employees are not aware of the existence of Wages Councils, and of their employers' obligations to them; third, the rate of prosecution, and the penalties imposed, when an abuse is found, are so low, that they do not act as a deterrent.

There is a further reason why Wages Councils have not given adequate protection to part-timers in particular. Minimum wages are currently given as a flat weekly amount, and this can be difficult for part-timers to interpret. However, Government proposals to introduce a single minimum hourly rate will overcome this difficulty.

The following is a list of the main industries covered by Wages Councils:

Aerated waters   Clothing and related
Catering   industries

Fur trade
Flax and hemp
Waste materials reclamation
Hairdressing
Lace finishing
Laundry
Millinery

Perambulator and invalid
car
Retail distribution
Rope, twine and net
Sack and bag
Toy manufacturing

At the time of writing (2nd edition, 1986) the Conservative Government had set in motion plans to remove all young people under 21 from the protection of Wages Councils, and to confine Wages Councils to setting only a single minimum hourly rate and a single overtime rate for those over 21. There are also rumours that the Wages Councils may eventually be abolished altogether, although no definite decisions have yet been made. This would imply that there is an urgent need for expansion and strengthening of trade union membership and activity in these sectors.

Information about Wages Councils can be obtained from the Central London Office (see p 188) or by phoning your local Wages Inspectorate.

Contracts of Employment
Every employee has a contract of employment with his or her employer from the moment of starting work, but not all contracts are explicit or written down. A contract of employment is a legal agreement between you and your employer which defines your rights and conditions and sets down your obligations to each other. It draws together everything described previously in this chapter which is relevant to your particular employment situation, and states the nature of your work. The contract of employment is particularly important because it is the basis upon which your employee status rests (see p 26) and it is the means of establishing continuity of employment.

As nothing need be set down in writing for a contract of employment to exist, it may be difficult to establish whether you have such a contract, and furthermore, to establish whether the contract, if you have one, is continuous or subject to constant termination and renewal. These are important matters for workers who need to be sure of their employee status, and who need to maintain a record of continuous employment.

If you work for more than 16 hours a week, however, it is your statutory right to have a written statement of your terms and conditions of employment. This is not, in itself, a contract of employment, but it will determine that such a contract exists, and will state its terms. The law says that the statement should contain the following details:

☐ Name of employer and employee
☐ The date employment began
☐ A rate of pay and interval between payments (weekly or monthly)
☐ Hours of work
☐ Holidays and holiday pay, if any
☐ Sick pay, if any
☐ Pension and pension scheme, if any
☐ Length of notice
☐ Rights in relation to trade union membership
☐ Grievance procedure, if any
☐ Disciplinary procedure, if any
☐ Title of your job

A statement of terms and conditions is particularly useful in identifying those benefits beyond the statutory minimum which your employer is willing to extend to you, but the extent to which the statement is a formal one, with everything accounted for in the small print, may depend on the size and nature of the organisation for which you work. Small employers, having a lot of personal contact with their employees, may dislike setting everything down in writing, and it may be tactless for you to require your employer to do so. In a large establishment you will be much better off if everything is clearly stated.

If you work for less than 16 hours, you are not entitled to a written statement, though an employer who is in the habit of dealing in them, may give you one regardless. This aspect of the law seems particularly unhelpful, as it is those part-time workers who have the most limited statutory rights who need a clear statement of their terms of employment.

State Benefits

There is a whole range of State benefits which is separate from the benefits employees obtain from their employers on the basis of their employment rights. There is, however, a degree of interaction between the two, as financial benefits received through employers can, in some cases, be reduced by the amount of any State benefits received. State benefits are

generally administered by the DHSS and are, unlike employment rights, theoretically available to everyone, whether they
are employed or unemployed. They are, however, inextricably
linked to employment, as eligibility for benefits is in most cases
dependent both on working patterns and on payments of
National Insurance contributions which are calculated as a
proportion of each person's income. There are in addition two
major sources of benefit which are currently available regardless
of the amount of National Insurance contributions paid. (The
system is due to be altered in 1988 — see also p 47.)

Family Income Supplement
Family Income Supplement (FIS) does not depend on National
Insurance contributions. Anyone can claim it as long as their
income is low enough and their working hours are right. It is the
major source of additional support for low wage-earning families
with children under 16 (and is also paid for children under 19
who are in full-time non-advanced education), but a grave
inequity is to be found in the rules relating to it. FIS is only
available to people who work for at least 24 hours a week in a
one-parent family and for 30 hours if there are two parents.
This discriminates against part-timers generally, and particularly
against couples who have decided to share childcare by both
taking part-time jobs. The working hours of a couple cannot be
added together, so if they each work for under 30 hours a week
they receive no benefit even if their combined wages are low
enough to make them otherwise eligible. (The situation will
change in 1988 when the new system of Family Credit is
introduced — see below.)
    You are eligible for FIS if your normal gross weekly income
is below the following: £86 plus £11.50 for each child under
11; £12.50 for each child aged 11-15; £13.50 for each child of
16 or over (November 1985 figures). In calculating your weekly
income, you should include any maintenance you receive if you
are a single parent, but *not* the amount you receive in State
Child Benefit, one parent benefit, your children's income (other
than maintenance payments), or any help you get with rent or
rates. If you get Supplementary Benefit you do not need to
FIS 1, from the Post Office, your local DHSS office, or a
community advice centre if there is one near where you live.

Supplementary Benefit
Supplementary Benefit is the one benefit designed especially

for part-time workers. It tops up the very low incomes of part-timers or people whose sole income is from benefits, but the amount you can claim is very much lower than that you could claim in FIS. If you or your partner work, you must work for fewer than 30 hours a week to claim Supplementary Benefit. The system of allowances is too complex to set down here as a separate amount is set for everyone in the family, varying with the ages of the children and with any special needs dependents may have. On this basis, the maximum for which you are eligible is calculated and then reduced by the amount of income you have from any source, whether earnings or benefits. You are then eligible for the sum arrived at by this method. As an example, a two-parent family with three children aged 8, 10 and 12 are eligible for a maximum of £100.30 (long-term rate) each week. Owner occupiers and certain other claimants get help with their housing costs, apart from rent and rates, through Supplementary Benefit. All help with rent and rates is generally provided for under the housing benefits scheme.

Single parents under 16 cannot claim Supplementary Benefit, and neither can people who have savings of more than £3,000.

Like Family Income Supplement, Supplementary Benefit is not dependent on payment of National Insurance contributions. To apply for benefit, you must obtain Form SB 1 from your post office, DHSS office, or local Community Advice Centre.

Housing Benefit
Housing Benefit is a scheme for providing help with rent and rates. If you get Supplementary Benefit you do not need to apply separately as the DHSS will send a 'certificate' to the local authority who will adjust your rent and/or rates automatically. You will normally get 100 per cent help with your rent and rates, unless for example you have someone living with you, such as a grown-up son or daughter or a lodger, or your rent includes the cost of services such as heating.

If you do not get Supplementary Benefit, perhaps because your income is a little too high to qualify, or you have savings of more than £3,000, you may still get help with housing costs. You can get help whether you own your own home, or live in accommodation owned by the local authority or a private landlord.

The exact calculation of housing benefit is rather complicated, but the amount of benefit will depend on four things:

☐ Your income
☐ The size of your family
☐ The amount of rent and/or rates you pay
☐ Whether anyone else (such as a lodger or a grown-up son or daughter) lives with you.

Although most income is taken into account in full (for example Child Benefit or FIS), certain types of income such as mobility or attendance allowance are ignored completely. Only part of some others is taken into account — for example, the first £17.30 of earnings is ignored.

Unlike social security benefits, Housing Benefit is administered by local authorities. If you wish to apply for Housing Benefit, you should obtain a claim form from your local council.

Proposals for Reform of Social Security

Norman Fowler's White Paper, *Reform of Social Security*, published December 1985, promised a thorough overhaul of the social security system, with the aim of directing resources towards 'areas of greatest need, notably low-income families with children'. Among other proposals, Family Income Supplement will be replaced by a new Family Credit Scheme; and Supplementary Benefit will be replaced by a new system of Income Support. These changes will be introduced in 1988.

The new system will be simpler, and one point for part-timers to bear in mind is that a single definition of 'regular work' — 24 hours a week — will apply as far as benefits are concerned. Above 24 hours a week, Family Credit can be claimed; below, Income Support (in the case of couples, both partners will have to be working for less than 24 hours a week to qualify for Income Support).

National Insurance Contributions

In the past it was usual for married women to claim benefits through their husbands and therefore opt out of paying National Insurance contributions on their own account, or pay at the reduced married women's rate. This practice has now been discontinued and, apart from some women who 'opted out' before 1977, everyone pays National Insurance contributions at the full rate. This is to the advantage of women as the benefits a wife can claim through her husband are less favourable than those she can claim in her own right. A woman cannot, for instance, claim maternity allowance, which is payable for

18 weeks, unless she does so in her own right, although all women receive a maternity grant (currently £25.00) if their husbands' National Insurance contributions are sufficient.

There are two arrangements for compulsory payment of National Insurance contributions: Class I for those people whose employment is provided by a single employer (in this case, both employer and employee contribute) and Class II and Class IV contributions for self-employed people who have no one employer to contribute on their behalf. There is a further arrangement which people who are 'non-employed' can elect to participate in. This is known as Class III and is a flat rate weekly payment which provides eligibility for some benefits.

All people who work full- or part-time for a single employer, whether they have employee status or not, must pay Class I contributions if their weekly earnings are more than £38.00 (April 1986). This rule also applies to people who work in two part-time jobs concurrently. The minimum level is set annually in April. Under this system, the employee pays a percentage of his or her income (calculated on a sliding scale according to the amount earned) and the employer also pays a percentage based on the employee's earnings.

Self-employed people are subject to different arrangements as they do not, in most cases, have a regular employer who can contribute on their behalf. Workers whose annual earnings are likely to be below £2,075 (April 1986) do not need to pay National Insurance contributions, but they must apply in advance for exemption by completing Form CF10 in leaflet NI 27A, obtainable from their local Social Security Office. Workers who earn more than £2,075 a year pay Class II contributions at the flat rate of £3.75 a week. Class IV contributions are a levy of 6.3 per cent on any income between £4,450 and £14,450 a year. (1986 figures.)

Self-employed people do rather better than those who pay Class I contributions as they are eligible for benefits in the same way as employees, but pay National Insurance contributions at a lower rate. However, State benefits may be of limited help as a substitute for employment rights.

ELIGIBILITY FOR BENEFIT

The basis for establishing eligibility for most benefits is the continuous payment of full contributions over a set period of time. To claim full unemployment benefit, maternity allowance, invalidity allowance and certain other benefits, a claimant must have paid 50 full National Insurance contributions in the preceding tax year. Such continuity can be difficult for part-timers to achieve, but, apart from this, the State benefits system does not discriminate against part-time workers as there is no 'hours worked' stipulation except for people claiming Family Income Supplement and Supplementary Benefit. What matters is the *number* of contributions, not their amount. The system is, however, geared to full-time workers, and part-timers may well suffer for this reason.

Part-timers are more likely than full-timers to lack employment protection and benefits, and therefore more likely to resort to the State benefits system to make up for these losses. Unfortunately, they are also more likely to have irregular working arrangements and for this reason they may, on technicalities, miss out on the benefits of both systems. The following letter and reply, published in the *Guardian* on 5 February 1983, is a good example of the way in which this can happen..

'I am a part-time teacher. I work at several colleges and am paid at an hourly rate. I am on a week's notice. I have no written contract. Last vacation, I applied for unemployment benefit. It was refused. The reason given: "The period from 16.12.82 to 8.1.83 is a period of recognised or customary holiday in connection with the claimant's employment". Does this also rule out unemployment benefit during the three-month summer vacation? My employment will end at about the middle of June.'

'It looks like it. Obviously, you have been classed as a seasonal worker, employed for only part of the year and at about the same time each year. This time is known as "the season". With breaks of seven weeks or more, and an established seasonal work pattern, you can only qualify if unemployed during your normal working season. You have appeal rights, but I am not very hopeful. Leaflet NI 55 gives you an outline of your position under these special rules.'

There are many individual cases of this nature, each one slightly different, and it would be impossible to attempt a comprehensive survey in this book. There are, however, a few disadvantages within the State benefits system which are experienced by large numbers of part-time workers, and these deserve attention.

Low Wage Earners

Many part-timers are on low incomes and when this coincides with working as a non-employee, as it often does, the temptation to conceal earnings and so avoid paying National Insurance contributions may be very great. Avoidance leads to two major disadvantages. It deprives people of benefits and, through the necessity to maintain concealment, forces them into accepting, without protest, terms and conditions of work which may be poor and can sometimes be frankly exploitative.

Very low wage earners are excluded from benefits because they earn too little to pay National Insurance contributions. Paying workers wages below the lower limit of £38.00 per week is obviously an attractive proposition for employers who wish to avoid paying their share, and the most unscrupulous among them may pay part-timers a wage just below the threshold — often with the agreement of the employee who is pleased to have no deductions. Married women can still obtain some benefits through their husbands, as long as their husbands' National Insurance contributions are sufficient, but these are fewer than the benefits they would obtain on their own account. If on the other hand, they have no husbands, they are largely unprotected. This is a situation which presents serious problems.

Unemployment Benefit
Part-timers are again at a disadvantage in claiming unemployment benefit. Looking for part-time work can be regarded as placing a 'restriction on the nature or conditions of work they are willing to accept', and if it is considered that, as a consequence, they have no reasonable prospects of getting work, unemployment benefit may not be payable. Unemployed part-timers should consult Leaflet NI 242 which can be obtained from any Unemployment Benefit Office.

State Retirement Pension
The size of your income over a sustained period is of far-reaching consequence when considering retirement pension. Everyone who pays full National Insurance contributions over nine-tenths of their working lives (16-65 for men, and 16-60 for women) receives a State Retirement Pension. Here, the State discriminates only against assumed idleness, because men and women can have payments credited to them for time off work for full-time study, or to care for other people, for example, children. Higher wage-earners are entitled to an Earnings Related addition or Additional Pension, according to the amount of their National Insurance contributions which are, of course, dependent on the size of their incomes. The Additional Pension will, when the Fowler proposals are implemented, be calculated on lifetime average earnings. People who reduce their income

for any length of time by working part-time will have this reflected in a smaller Additional Pension.

Many employers have a company pension or superannuation scheme and although these fall more correctly into the category of negotiated benefits, it seems logical to deal with them here as they may affect workers' eligibility within the State scheme. If you contribute to a company scheme which satisfies certain requirements your employer may contract you out of the State Additional Pension. The company scheme then becomes responsible for providing you with a pension which must not be less than what is known as the guaranteed minimum pension (GMP). The GMP is a substitute for, and broadly equivalent to, the State Additional Pension. In return for providing a GMP both the employer and you will pay a smaller National Insurance contribution. You must pay National Insurance contributions to qualify for a GMP. You will normally be required to pay contributions to your employer's scheme. Company schemes usually offer terms which are more advantageous than those obtained from the State Additional Pension but rely heavily on length and amount of contributions, which are linked to wage levels. If you intend to stay with the same employer for most of your working life, it is certainly worth becoming contracted-out if the opportunity arises. If you envisage changes of employer, the advantages are less certain as part-timers are often excluded from company schemes. However, if you have left employment on or after 1 January 1986 you have the right to a transfer value which is the cash equivalent of the pension rights you have built up in the company scheme. This can be used to buy you rights in any new employer's scheme that will accept it or to buy an annuity with an insurance company of your choice. Alternatively you can choose a combination of both. You can, of course, leave your pension rights with your former company scheme and if you do so, schemes are required to revalue certain parts of such rights. Whichever way you decide, your eligibility to a State basic Retirement Pension is unchanged.

As private schemes involve the employer in financial contributions, it is common for employers to make savings by excluding part-timers from pension schemes. A half-way position is to exclude them unless they specifically ask to make contributions. Either way, you need to be sure what the position is, and, if it discriminates against you, you can ask your union for help, if you belong to one. People most badly affected by exclusion are those who, as full-time workers, previously contributed, and as part-timers are barred from doing so. But if you are put in such a position on or after 1 January 1986, you have the same right to a transfer value as someone leaving employment.

Conclusion

Part-timers generally are in a weak position regarding their employment, and are most disadvantaged if they lack eligibility for employment rights for any of the following reasons: because they do not have employee status; because they work for less than 16 hours a week; because they work in a firm employing fewer than six workers or because frequent job changes prevent them from establishing the continuity of employment needed to qualify for rights and benefits. Part-timers are also less likely to be appointed as permanent staff. Although legally the term 'permanent employee' is virtually meaningless, as no employer can be held liable in law to retain the services of an employee for ever, it is nevertheless a term used to distinguish employees whose potential length of employment is open-ended from those who are engaged on a temporary or fixed-term basis. Self-employed people, of course, are not eligible for any of these benefits and rights, and they should note that State benefits are not an adequate substitute for them.

Workers who are aware of their rights are less likely to allow themselves to be deprived of them. For instance, they will try to stop their hours being reduced to below the 16 hour minimum, or their wages falling below the National Insurance threshold. Membership of a trade union is a safeguard as most unions will advise and act on behalf of part-timers when requested to do so. It is also, all round, a safer proposition to be employed in a large firm rather than in a small one.

However, the fact remains that insecure forms of employment are often the most readily available, and are significantly more convenient, for the person who needs to work part-time. Further aspects of this problem are discussed in Chapter 3.

Forms of Part-time Employment

Introduction

Lack of employee status is a significant feature of part-time work. Those who lack employee status are generally referred to as being self-employed, although the term used in this sense is somewhat misleading. There are various forms of employment which do not usually carry employee status (see p 26), most notably homeworking, freelancing or *specific* self-employment (eg running a small enterprise, or joining in partnership or group practice with other self-employed people). Most people who work under arrangements of this sort are regarded as independent workers, not employees.

Full-timers who choose self-employment usually do so because of the nature of their occupation, or because they have sufficient resources to take an independent initiative. They therefore make the decision from a position of strength. Part-timers, on the other hand, often find that self-employment is their *only* option. They may be unable to find a part-time post, or to work the hours required, or they may need to work at home. They therefore opt to be independent and unprotected from a position of need rather than strength, and they are often unaware that they might be able to establish the employee status they are denied if they sought a legal judgement. In view of the proportionately larger number of part-timers than full-timers who work without employment protection, due note should be taken of whether the various forms of employment described below tend to carry employee status or not.

Temporary Work

Much part-time work is of a temporary nature, and most employers do not regard temporary workers as employees. Contract work, seasonal and agency work is usually readily available in a wide range of occupations. Temps are in demand, particularly for nursing, clerical and secretarial duties. These temps may have some difficulty in deciding their employment status, and almost all will effectively be denied their rights under employment law if their periods of work with one employer do not last long enough for them to establish sufficient continuity of employment (see p 33). In general, there is no reason why temporary workers should not be regarded as employees as long as they are engaged to work by the employer concerned, and cannot in any sense be regarded as independent contractors − for instance, by using their own materials and equipment or by employing assistants on their own account. In practice, however, few temporary workers enjoy the benefits of being an employee. Many are engaged through agencies. In these cases the employer cannot be said to have made a contract of employment with the worker. Many more are deemed to be independent on technicalities, and few stay long enough for the question to be relevant. If you do find yourself remaining for long with one employer, however, it is worth while arguing that custom and practice have established that you are an employee.

Although temporary work rarely constitutes permanent employment, it can be a useful way of making contacts which might lead to a permanent appointment. It can also ease you back into working if you have not been working for a while, and give you some up-to-date experience.

The easiest way to find temporary work is through an employment agency. You will be able to state your requirements − the hours you wish to work; how far you are willing to travel; and the kind of job you want to do.

In 1986, Reed Employment carried out a survey among 3,000 of their registered temps, which came up with some interesting points. It emerged that freedom and flexibility were important reasons for temping; and over 25 per cent of those completing the questionnaire chose temporary work as a way of testing the job market, before committing themselves to permanent employment. An insignificant number had chosen temping 'just for the money'.

The survey also found that temps were being asked to do work of increasing complexity − a contrast with the situation in the past, when temps were often employed for mundane chores, such as filing.

Reed Employment's survey (admittedly limited to their own temporary staff) found that 90 per cent of temporaries enjoy the same benefits — such as holiday pay — as permanent employees.

The agency foresees a substantial future expansion of temporary work, with as many as 80 per cent of office workers being employed on a temporary or contract basis by the year 2000.

The advantage of temporary work seems to be convenience and availability. Occasionally you may be offered a permanent appointment, and it may be possible for you to negotiate the hours worked and turn the position into the part-time job you need (see p 104), but more often temping means just that. Use it as a stepping stone but, if possible, do not do it for too long.

Part-time Employment

In the field of permanent employment, part-time work is the most usual arrangement. This usually means that you are an *employee* at a particular workplace, but you work for less than the standard number of hours worked by your full-time colleagues at that establishment. You are entitled to protection under the basic provisions of employment law and to all the statutory benefits for which you qualify by reason of your working hours and length of employment (see Chapter 2), but there is no guarantee that, beyond this, you will be treated *pro rata* on a par with equivalent full-time colleagues.

Part-time work is usually arranged in shifts or sessions, which may involve working a reduced number of hours each day, or a reduced number of full days each week — or a combination of the two. It is normally initiated by the employer to suit his or her needs, but employers who rely heavily on part-timers necessarily tailor their demands to the likely sources of labour, and, in many cases, create working shifts which fit in with family life. These are most likely to be a shortened day, for example from 10.00 am until 3.00 pm, or early morning and evening shifts when fathers are likely to be at home to take over domestic tasks. These arrangements are obviously made with women in mind and will therefore most commonly be found in 'women's' work, notably retail distribution, domestic and catering work, and assembly and packaging in manufacturing industries. They are less common in offices, although in small businesses sympathetic employers are to be found who will accommodate the needs of an employee they value. In large offices a different system is well-established, which will be described below (see job-splitting).

In occupations which, by their nature, offer little flexibility in hours, working time will be dictated by the demands of the job. School teachers must teach while the children are at school; GPs must practise when the surgery is open. In such situations, part-timers are appointed to work a certain number of sessions and there is no possibility of negotiating when these sessions begin and end. The same can be true in occupations where there are peak periods of activity, for instance lunch hours, late opening nights and weekends in shops and building societies. These are the times, whether convenient or not, when counter assistants will be most in demand.

There is a whole selection of jobs which are only available on a part-time basis because the work to be done does not occupy the full working day or week. Working hours are not flexible, but may, in many cases, be convenient as they are contained within the school day. School crossings patrol, parks and playground attendants, school cooks and dinner helpers are examples of people employed in this way. Such jobs have the advantage of being clear-cut. You know precisely what your hours and duties are from the outset and you cannot be 'put upon' or accused of taking full-timers' jobs. But there may be serious disadvantages such as a lack of holiday or sick pay, and work in these areas is among the most vulnerable in the present climate of cuts in public spending.

Job-splitting

In office work, which is less easily adapted to part-time working patterns of shifts or sessions, the practice of job-splitting, or 'twinning', has established itself over a great many years. This is a system by which an employer decides to split one full-time job into two or more parts and engage different people to do it, so that together they provide full-time cover across each working week. This has the advantage for the employer of ensuring maximum use of office space and equipment, as the job partners share the same desk and machines. As each will be at work when the other is not, problems can be encountered if much communication is needed to link the various parts of the job. In routine clerical and administrative work, however, where job-splitting is most commonly practised, this is not usually the case and jobs can effectively be broken down into separate, self-contained units.

Job-splitting opportunities are most common in large offices such as those of the major clearing banks and insurance companies. Patterns of work will be well established and it will not normally be possible to negotiate individual arrangements. The method of dividing working hours can change from one employer to another, but a popular arrangement is a system of working alternate weeks. This may be of little use to the mother of young children who needs to be at home for a part of each day, but many people who simply need more free hours than a full-time job affords will find they can adapt to it. Many already have — Barclays' Bank has 9,000 auxiliary office staff, of which a proportion work on alternate weeks.

Job partners are usually appointed as permanent employees. However, despite the fact that employers appoint them to fill a full-time post and therefore, presumably, expect a quality of work equal to that of a full-timer, they still treat them essentially as part-time staff, in terms of the benefits, conditions and prospects they are offered. Some concessions may be made beyond those accorded to ordinary part-timers, but these do not give job partners parity with their full-time colleagues. Barclays' Bank, for instance, gives all its job-split workers the same maternity leave and rate of pay as full-timers, and the same paid holidays *pro rata*, but reduced entitlement to sick leave and no opportunity to participate in the Bank's pension scheme. This type of discrimination is reflected in the arrangements of most of the major employers who use job-splitting systems.

For administrative purposes, each job partner is treated as an individual employee, although each shares the same job. Each has his or her own employment contract, salary and benefits arrangements which will relate to individual circumstances and are unaffected by those of his or her partner. In most matters, job partners are in the same position as ordinary part-time employees and must fulfil the same criteria to qualify for benefits. Difficulties have arisen, however, for people working alternate weeks, over establishing continuity of employment. Fortunately for those contemplating this form of working, precedents have now been set which safeguard their interests in law.

In 1978, an employee of Lloyd's Bank, working alternate weeks, was in danger of losing her right to maternity leave unless she could establish that her work arrangements constituted 'continuing employment'. A case was brought before the Employment Appeal Tribunal and a ruling made that, where a period of absence from the workplace is by arrangement and the employee is regarded as continuing in the employment of his or her employer, that period shall count as a period of employment. Thus, continuity has been established as long as the employee has a continuing employment contract. This is an important point, as it is not unknown for employers to disengage and re-engage part-timers working on/off schedules to avoid their obligations to them in law.

In this same case, it also became necessary to establish the time qualification, needed by a person working alternate weeks, to become eligible for benefit. Should the person concerned, for instance, work double the number of years as only half the possible number of weeks were worked in any one year? Again, a ruling was made that, as the weeks away from the workplace were regarded in law as periods of employment, the length of continuous employment was that which had elapsed since the employee had taken up his or her appointment.

Now that these points have been established, there seem to be no hidden snags in the job-splitting system beyond those which any part-timer with employee status would encounter, and there is one anomalous advantage. If you work alternate weeks, you are protected under employment law if you are employed for 16 hours or more *on the weeks when you work*. You are thus in a better position than many part-timers working every week for less than 16 hours. Spread evenly over a period of time their hours may average more than yours, yet they have no protection.

For further details of job-splitting, see p 69 under Government-sponsored schemes.

Job-sharing

The practicalities of job-sharing are similar to those of job-splitting in that it involves two or more employees combining to do one full-time job, but the ideology behind the two systems is different. Job-splitting is initiated by the employer, usually to ease staff shortages caused by a lack of full-time employees. Job-sharing can be initiated by either the employer or the employee, but, either way, it is employee-orientated in its intentions.

The aims of job-share schemes are twofold: to open up part-time jobs in occupations where few have been available previously, and to extend to part-timers the advantages accorded to full-time workers. Nothing can alter the position of job-sharers in law, as this is dependent on hours worked and continuity of employment, but there are many other aspects of part-time employment in which part-timers are discriminated against. Job-sharing can and does go a long way to improve this situation.

Part-timers have, as has already been described (see Chapter 2) fewer statutory and negotiated rights. They are also limited in matters of status and promotion, as is shown in Chapter 4 (pp 80-86). The rationale behind job-sharing is that, if the principle of job-sharers participating in a *full-time* post is strictly adhered to, such limitations should not occur.

The Inner London Education Authority (ILEA), which is generally regarded as a forward-looking and liberal authority, recently agreed to set up a pilot scheme under which 60 teachers were allowed to share 30 teaching posts. The Authority already permits job-sharing for its non-teaching staff.

Most job-sharing schemes at present are found within the public sector. In London, for instance, it has spread most rapidly in the local authorities. The now-defunct GLC, committed to giving equal opportunities to all its workers, agreed a policy that opened up job-sharing to most of its 22,000 employees.

Hackney Council, which set up a job-sharing policy several years ago, now has 40 employees sharing 20 jobs. As part of this policy, the council put a letter in the pay packets of all its employees, informing them of their right to job-share. The council has also been running a series of training seminars, with the assistance of Hackney Job Share Project, to explain the policy and its implementation to management.

Camden Council has adopted a job-sharing project which has led to 30 jobs being shared by 60 employees. Recently the council held seminars for these sharers to discuss their experiences and identify any improvements needed to the system. Camden and Hackney also run their own registers to match prospective job sharers with suitable partners wherever possible.

There are formal job-sharing policies or arrangements for sharing jobs in Brent, Barnet, Ealing, Hammersmith and Fulham, Harrow, Waltham Forest and Lewisham. Some of these councils also publicly advertise certain jobs as open to sharing. Negotiations are currently taking place to establish job-sharing policies in Southwark, Greenwich and Haringey, which already employ sharers, and in Hounslow. Other boroughs such as Westminster and Islington have employed job sharers despite the absence of a formal agreement.

Some of the types of council jobs being shared in London include clerical officers, telephonists, receptionists, planners, social workers, administrative assistants and librarians.

While no large private employer in London has yet adopted a job-sharing policy, it is not unusual for employees who want to work fewer hours while staying in the same job to negotiate individual job-sharing arrangements. Where no company policy exists, joint applications to share an advertised full-time job vacancy can be made. Private sector jobs currently being shared in London include the training manager of the Stock Exchange, bank clerks and BBC production assistants and secretaries.

Outside London, a notable example of a local authority committed to job sharing is Sheffield City Council, and Sheffield Education Authority has extended the opportunity to teachers. There are currently about 115 teachers working job-share schemes. In these cases, all posts are advertised as being open to job-sharers unless it is felt that the responsibilities of a particular post could not be undertaken in this way.

As long ago as 1969, the DHSS sent a directive to hospital authorities requiring them to 'actively encourage' married women doctors to return to work. One of the suggestions offered was to split '. . . existing posts *which have proved difficult to fill on a whole-time basis* (author's italics) into two or more part-time appointments where this is consistent with service needs.' This directive is firmly within the spirit of job-splitting. The Lothian Health Board, to its credit, took up the challenge and turned it into what has become a model job-share scheme. Since 1975, the Board has made provision for two people rather than one, as extras paid in employers' from house officer to consultant. The job-sharers are given considerable freedom to arrange the sharing to their convenience and conditions of employment appear to be fair (see Appendix B, pp 177-178).

Apart from such enlightened employers, and, to a certain extent, in relation to them, too, the onus is on the would-be job-sharer to convince the employer that the arrangement will work. Two important prerequisites are the compatibility of the job-sharers and their ability to link the two halves of the job without any breakdown in communication. It should be pointed out that there is little extra cost involved in employing two people rather than one, as extras paid in employers' National Insurance contributions and the administration of two files rather than one are negligible. Conversely, there are positive benefits as job-sharers commonly cover each other's leave, help out in emergencies such as sickness, and provide job continuity in the event of one sharer leaving before the other.

There are various ways in which you can persuade an employer, who may have no experience of job-sharing, to appoint you on that basis. All ways take some courage and initiative, but the rewards, if you are successful, will make it worth while. First, it is advisable to find a suitable sharer, as an individual approach to an employer is almost certainly doomed to failure. Even as a pair you may be viewed with suspicion if the arrangement is a new one for the employer, so finding temporary shared work through an employment agency might be to your advantage. It would enable you, as a pair, to try out the arrangement for yourselves and to apply for a permanent post with that experience in your favour. Probably the surest way to success is for you and someone else in your firm to negotiate with your present employer to change to a job-share arrangement, but this is only possible when an opportunity arises — for instance, a promotion which would normally be denied to a part-timer; or your own wish to change from full- to part-time working without losing your responsibilities or status.

At the present time job-sharing is confined mainly to people in professional jobs, but there is no reason why almost any work should not be done in this way. With the onus on the sharers to decide on time arrangements which suit them, it promises more flexibility in working hours than any other form of employment at a workplace. At its best, it would provide a structure in which sharers could mutually support each other through difficult times, whilst maintaining the quality of their work and, therefore, their credibility with both employers and colleagues. Job-sharing might also, to some extent, solve the present insoluble problem, so often mentioned by interviewees: of what to do about the children during school holidays.

Because job-sharing is considered to be an important new initiative an information and advice network has grown up, and literature is available on the subject (see p 184). New Ways to Work, a job-sharing project in London, operates a computerised register to pair up job-sharers, and may be able to help people living outside London to contact a local job-share group, or to start one of their own.

Homeworking

Homeworking is, as it implies, work you do at home. Homeworkers usually work for only one firm and, by the nature of their work, are totally dependent on the employer for their ability to work. The employer provides them with the tasks, the materials for the work and, often, the necessary equipment. It is not work which they could do privately and on their own initiative. Despite these facts, which are consistent with employee status, homeworkers are not usually regarded as employees. Although the flow of work can be uneven, homeworking is usually regarded as a long-term proposition and many people remain with the same employer for years.

Traditional types of homework are mainly associated with the clothing and knitwear industries, and also with light assembly work such as toymaking. However, the last few years have also seen the emergence of a group that may be termed 'new homeworkers'. They usually work as computer professionals (or, in a minority of cases, in clerical work associated with the new technologies, such as word-processing or data entry). It is likely, with the advent of cable networks, that it will become increasingly cost-effective to employ clerical workers at home, and that this second group will expand significantly.

In 1982 a survey was conducted by the Equal Opportunities Commission, interviewing 78 homeworkers whose work involved the use of new technology. Their average pay levels were found to be significantly lower than the going rates for similar work on-site, and some of them (particularly those who were designated as self-employed) lacked a number of benefits available to on-site workers. Thus the new homeworkers may have more in common with 'traditional' homeworkers than might at first appear.

The obvious advantages of homeworking are that it does not take you away from home and you can regulate the amount of work you do and the times when you do it. This makes it an attractive proposition if you have the care of young children or elderly relatives, or if your health makes it difficult for you to get about. Once you are settled with an employer, you will have your work delivered to you regularly and collected when you have completed it. Your wages, too, may be brought to you at home.

There are, however, serious drawbacks to homeworking. First, you will have the task of organising yourself and coping with the paraphernalia of your work, which may take up a considerable amount of space. Homeworkers in the 'traditional' sphere are paid piecework rates, so your earnings will depend on your speed and efficiency as well as your skill in doing the job. Research has found that most homeworkers earn very little in their first year, even if they have previous factory experience of the work they are doing, because of the problem of establishing a self-imposed rhythm of work amid the distractions of their homes. After that, if they stay the course, matters quickly improve and they attain a level of wage-earning which will probably remain fairly constant in the coming years, if work is available.

Yet 'high' levels of earning in one industry often bear no resemblance to those in another. Poor pay is the norm, and this is the second disadvantage that must be reckoned with. Although it is possible to earn good money in some jobs, this is by no means the general picture. A survey carried out by the Department of Employment in 1982 found 27 per cent of homeworkers earning a gross wage of less than £1 an hour. And nearly all of the homeworkers contacted by Dundee Inner City Action Centre in 1984 earned less than this amount. Even the 'new homeworkers' surveyed in 1982, who earned an average of £4.62 an hour, were paid significantly below the computer industry average, which at the time was £5.69 per hour.

If as a homeworkers you believe you are underpaid, you may have one form of protection. Some of the industries which employ homeworkers are covered by Wages Councils (see Chapter 2, p 42) and the statutory minimum pay rates apply to all workers, whether employed in the workplace or not. The complaints procedure described on p 42 is open to everybody.

However, the findings of research being carried out by the Low Pay Unit in 1983 suggest that homeworkers seldom complain about their working conditions and rates of pay. Of 52 homeworkers interviewed, a third earned 50p an hour or less and just over three-quarters earned £1 an hour or less. These figures fall well below the Low Pay Unit definition of low pay, which for 1983 stood at £2.25 an hour. They were also badly paid in relation to legal minimum wages. Machinists were entitled to receive £1.59 an hour in 1983 if they were pieceworkers: in fact the machinists in this survey were earning an average of 83.4p — barely half the legal minimum. The reasons for this apparently widespread acceptance of a bad lot are various. Many homeworkers may be unaware of their legal rights. Even if they are aware of them, they are isolated and in a bad position to take strength from group action. Or they may be unsure if they should be paying tax and insurance and reluctant to draw attention to themselves for this reason. The facts are that everybody earning above the lowest level (£44.90 single and £70.29 married for income tax and £38.00 for National Insurance — April 1986 figures) should pay contributions whether their employer deducts this at source or not. People earning below these amounts should sign a form of exemption, obtainable at local DHSS offices.

Probably the most overwhelming reason for the lack of complaints is the fear that, if they are 'awkward', employers will quite simply cease to employ them. This is quite easily done as homeworkers usually have no employment rights in law and therefore little opportunity of redress in cases of unfair dismissal. Although to all intents and purposes they are employees, depending upon an employer for the work they do, most employers prefer to regard them as self-employed as this releases them from all obligations except paying, on their terms, for work done. Thus, it is rare for homeworkers to get paid holidays, sick pay or maternity benefit. And in most cases they have no job security.

Yet the picture is not as bleak as it might seem. A Low Pay Unit pamphlet on homeworkers, entitled 'The Hidden Army' (1979) quotes three cases in which women homeworkers have brought cases before industrial tribunals to establish employee status, and have won. A more recent ruling has also widened the definition of 'employee' status; two homeworkers who had full discretion over the amount of work they accepted, and the pace at which they completed the work, were held to have had a relationship of 'employment' rather than 'self-employment' with the firm they worked for. From these examples, it seems probable that many homeworkers could win cases for employee status, though what is needed is an Act of Parliament establishing this. Reform is an important issue as homeworking is so undeniably an essential working arrangement for many people.

Recently, help has been available from the trade unions. Two unions, the National Union of Hosiery and Knitwear Workers and the National Union of Tailors and Garment Workers, have decided to include homeworkers in their wage negotiations, and the General and Municipal Workers' Union is pledged to active support for an improved deal for homeworkers. There are also various organisations committed to supportive and campaigning work (see Part 3, p 187). Homeworking, particularly in the new technology fields, is likely to increase in future. It is important that homeworkers should be granted employee status, and that they should have access to trade union organisations.

Freelancing

Freelancers, like homeworkers, are not normally regarded as employees and therefore do not often enjoy employment protection or benefits. They must exist on the payment for the work they do and will not receive paid holidays, sick pay, pension schemes, redundancy pay or maternity leave, or any other fringe benefits available to employees. Most freelancers are professional people and can usually command reasonable rates of pay for the work they do. Given sufficient demand for their services, freelancers can adjust their work flow to fit their personal circumstances, and this makes freelancing an ideal form of part-time work. If you work with words you should be able to find a place as a freelancer, though it can take some initiative and courage to find a market for your services, unless you are lucky enough to have useful contacts or a previous employer who can provide you with work. In addition to work of a literary nature — journalism, editing, writing, translating and indexing are among the commonest freelance occupations — accountants, secretaries, and anybody specialising in office or administrative procedures only occasionally required by small firms may also find work.

If you work at home, like any homeworker you must organise your work in your domestic setting. You are more likely, however, to be familiar with a working situation which requires self-management, and less likely to be burdened with cumbersome 'tools of trade' cluttering up your living space. You will not usually be paid any expenses, so must provide yourself with the materials and equipment you need. Usually these are minimal and should present no problem, but you may need advice about such matters as rates of pay, legal aspects of contracts and general work arrangements. There is a range of professional societies which cover most kinds of work undertaken by freelancers (see Part 3, p 187) and you should find one which can help.

On the debit side, you may feel isolated and unpleasantly detached from the finished product to which you have contributed. This is particularly likely to be the case if your work is only one part of a total process (for example, if you work as a freelance editor at home for a publishing firm), and particularly if you have previously worked on site with close contact with all stages of the job in hand. You may miss the relationship with colleagues and feel that you have been deprived of stimulus and a standard by which to judge the quality of your work. However, these matters are very much a question of personality and the type of work you like doing. You may well prefer to work by yourself away from the hurly burly of an office, and be grateful for the lack of constant interruptions to the work flow.

Another method of freelancing is to work mainly for one employer at his or her premises. If you do this, your main commitment is to this employer but you are also free to undertake additional work independently. You are essentially free to come and go as you please; to work or not to work; and to organise your work as you wish. This does not mean, of course, that you can take completely arbitrary decisions as to whether to work or not, or to be in the least undependable — nobody will continue to engage the services of a person who is unreliable or fails to meet deadlines — but it does give more room for self-determination for the freelancer than any employer/employee relationship.

As well as having responsibility for the manner in which the work is done, as a freelancer you have responsibility for all aspects of your financial remuneration — and this includes negotiating prices, chasing up poor payers and pressing for payment. Payment is at an agreed rate for each piece of work done, and is not usually made until the job is complete. As some jobs can last for weeks, or even months, you cannot expect a steady income. You are taxed as a self-employed person, and must manage your tax and insurance yourself or employ an accountant to do it for you. You may also be liable for VAT if your earnings are high enough.

Self-employment

Although all non-employees are self-employed (in the sense that they have no employer who is legally obliged to acknowledge his or her obligations towards them), most remain dependent on employers for their work. This is the case with freelancers and homeworkers. There is a further category of people, however, who do not have this dependence and they are *specifically* self-employed because they work for themselves, whether singly, in partnership, or in association with others.

If, for instance, you are a doctor or a dentist or a solicitor in general practice; if you run a market stall or set up as a music or ballet teacher, you offer a service directly to the public and there is no 'middle man' who commissions your work.

All self-employed people are responsible for the management of their own income tax and National Insurance contributions, and for paying VAT for which they may be liable if their earnings are high enough. They must also finance the expenses incurred through their work. Although tax and insurance matters must be managed on an individual basis, there are two ways of dealing with expenses. You can work alone and carry sole responsibility, or you can work in conjunction with other people and spread the load.

If you work alone, the burden can be considerable and the financial risks high, but if your work thrives you will enjoy complete autonomy to organise it as you wish. If, on the other hand, you work in a group you will probably have more financial security but will be subject to some constraints. There may be a group approach to the work done, with which you will need to comply, and there will almost certainly be internally agreed arrangements in such matters as division of income and contributions towards overheads. Even in a group composed of independent, self-employed workers, there may be an established order of precedence and responsibility ranging from 'partners', through 'associates' to 'junior associates', which affects the influence and even the financial rewards of each person.

Many self-employed people working in conjunction with others are paid a rate per item of work, in the same way as homeworkers and freelancers. Some groups, on the other hand, may, by personal arrangement, decide to divide profits proportionately among their members. Anyone receiving a *salary*, however, is not a self-employed person but an employee. However much security a group may create for its members, it must be remembered that arrangements made between one self-employed person and another break down if the business fails, and there is no outside source of protection. One condition holds good for all self-employed people: if the enterprise fails, there is no employer who can be held responsible.

New Initiatives and their Significance for Part-timers

Flexitime

Flexitime is an established system which gives workers the opportunity to vary their working hours within a structure set down by the employer. It is not a major feature of part-time working, having been conceived with full-timers in mind, but it deserves some attention as it seems, potentially, to offer an ideal solution to the problems many part-timers encounter. It first appeared in Britain in 1971, and though it may have influenced some employers to grant more flexibility to their part-timers on an informal basis it is only rarely applied systematically to part-time workers.

The principle of flexitime is that the workplace is open for longer than the standard working day. The working hours are divided into a 'core' section around the middle of the day, during which all employees must work, and 'flexible bands' in the early morning and late afternoon. Each worker can decide his or her own starting and finishing time, as long as the stipulated number of hours are worked. The system is, theoretically, extremely adaptable, ranging from limited flexibility within each day, through flexibility within a week or a month, to flexibility across a longer period, with opportunities to amass credit hours which may be used to take time off during normal working hours.

Part-timers are, almost by definition, people with heavier than usual outside-work commitments. As these can change from day to day and from week to week, the value of such flexibility in working hours is obvious. If flexitime were more widely available it would enable many people, who cannot work or who restrict themselves to temping, to seek permanent posts. It would also ease the lives of many more who find the rigid hours of even a part-time job difficult to manage.

Unfortunately, work on continuous operations, or work involving contact with the public, cannot usually be arranged in this way, so large numbers of part-time workers, notably in the service industries and health care, could not hope to benefit from flexitime arrangements. Despite these limitations, flexitime is thought to be more adaptable to a variety of occupations than its present applications indicate. Up to the present, it has been used mainly by insurance firms, local government and the public services for their white-collar workers. Part-timers may find it an arrangement most frequently offered to them by small, employee-orientated employers, particularly voluntary organisations with a concern for social welfare. Employers who have tried flexitime have generally considered it worthwhile, in spite of the extra administration it involves, and there has been a slow but steady expansion since its introduction into Britain 15 years ago. Little attention has been paid, however, to its value for part-timers. It may be considered as a method of working that part-timers might want to adopt in the future — a new initiative which might be taken up by employers in response to clearly articulated demands from individuals interested in flexitime arrangements.

Government Sponsored Schemes

In 1982 the Government announced two new schemes to ease the unemployment situation. The first was the job-splitting scheme under which a grant (£840 in April 1985) became payable to an employer when the splitting of a job resulted either in the recruitment of an unemployed person receiving benefit, or in the prevention of a redundancy. The second was the Community Programme which was due to provide 230,000 jobs by June 1986, 75 per cent of them part-time, each for a period of not more than a year. The jobs go to the long-term unemployed and will involve working on community schemes.

Unfortunately, these new moves are far from being an acknowledgement of the need to open up more part-time jobs for people who wish to work part-time, and any benefit part-timers derive from the schemes will be purely incidental. The temporary nature of the community scheme debars it from consideration as a source of permanent employment, and seems designed simply to take people off the unemployment register (and therefore out of unemployment statistics) for a while. A few people might gain interests and skills which might lead on to permanent employment, but it would be optimistic to hope that these will be more than a very small number.

The people most likely to benefit from the job-splitting scheme are those nearing retirement who sometimes seek part-time work to ease them out of their working life. They may now have the opportunity to remain with their present employer in a job-split. There is also a slight chance that the financial incentives offered to employers may work in favour of people who propose to job-share, but, in the main, those who are actively seeking to work part-time will find themselves ineligible to benefit from these schemes.

Chapter 4

Making the Decision:
Factors which Influence the Quality
of Part-time Work

Introduction

Part-time work is a subject which has, so far, been under-researched, though it has received some attention within the more general context of women's employment. Elias and Main (1982) revealed in some detail patterns of part-time working in Britain, but the authors, on their own admission, lacked the data to research a number of important aspects. They were unable to draw conclusions about the effect of part-time working on the work history of individuals, to relate working patterns to exact family circumstances, or to make any assessment of the levels of job-satisfaction achieved through part-time work. All these aspects are important and, in the absence of any structured information, the best a prospective part-timer can do is to be guided by the experience of others.

With this in mind, Part 2 of this book was planned around 32 case studies, which are personal statements by people involved in a wide range of part-time occupations. From these accounts, a number of facts emerged which seemed to have a strong bearing on whether or not the work experience was satisfactory. There seemed to be a number of influences which combined to colour an employee's view of his or her work, in which those relating to personal circumstances could be as important as those deriving from the job.

Parents who had adequate childcare arrangements, and no worries about the care of their children during school holidays, tended to find their jobs more satisfactory than those who did not. People who were allowed flexibility in working arrangements to cope with family crises also felt the quality of their employment to be enhanced. Although many were financially dependent on their earnings, surprisingly few deplored the low pay they received. Dissatisfactions centred mainly around the job itself — where this was felt to be unworthy of their skills and experience, or where part-timers were viewed by colleagues or employer to be 'marginal' and subject to different pressures and expectations than full-timers.

Positive job satisfaction was mentioned as often as the lack of it, and derived from several sources. An important factor here, in view of the humble status of so many part-time jobs, was each person's previous work experience, and consequent acceptance or non-acceptance of the status conferred by their part-time employment. In general, job satisfaction was related to the extent of autonomy the part-timer had, and the degree to which he or she could feel responsible for a complete job done. Variety in work tasks was also considered to be an advantage and contributed to the satisfaction felt.

The sociability of the work situation was also important. Most people who sought work for social reasons were happy with the work they found.

A few of the people interviewed had consciously considered their part-time employment in the context of a whole working life. Others had vague thoughts for the future, but most appeared to be living in the present and taking each day as it came. The evidence (Elias and Main, 1982) suggests that part-time working is, for most people, a temporary arrangement, sandwiched between periods of full-time work and often preceded by some years away from work during childbearing. This chapter, therefore, will consider the effects of the career break, and of part-time work, in the context of a whole working life, as well as discussing those factors which seem to have a major bearing on whether or not the experience of being a part-timer is satisfactory.

Childcare

The problem of combining the demands of work with the needs of children, and with the needs of parents to feel satisfied with the way they carry out their parental caring, was probably the most dominant problem arising from the interviews. It seems sensible, therefore, if you are a parent contemplating part-time work, to examine the childcare options open to you, and your own feelings about making use of them.

Despite 20 years of increasing employment opportunities for married women, and a radical change during this time in the composition of many families, parents are given little help and no encouragement to abandon their traditional roles. Lack of childcare facilities and flexible working patterns still keep many mothers at home and almost all fathers (except the unemployed) at work. Despite a growing voice of protest, prevailing attitudes deem this situation to be 'right'. Little serious attention is given to campaigns for paternity leave, to job-sharing schemes enabling both mother and father to care for their children, or to the creation of part-time jobs which would enable more women to work.

The debate between women working and staying at home has centred upon the pre-school years of the children and has therefore tended to mask the extent of the problem. It inclines people to think in terms of a period of five years, which is unrealistic for an average family with two or more children whose ages span some years. The mother who decides to stay at home until all her children are at school will usually find herself away from work for much longer than five years and will have diminished her employment prospects in the process. Even when children start school, they do not become magically self-sufficient outside school hours. For a long while to come, a decision to work part-time may be the only decision if mothers are to work at all.

There are several forms of childcare for pre-school children. Council day nurseries, private or workplace nurseries, child-minders, playgroups, school nurseries, nannies or other private arrangements are possible solutions to childcare problems. But it would be misleading to suggest that working parents are often presented with a choice. Some of these facilities are available only to people with special needs; others may offer hours which do not suit or which may be unavailable in the particular area. The most ideal may be too expensive, and the most logical for working parents — workplace nurseries — are rarely provided.

The social services departments of local authorities run day nurseries, but these are reserved for priority cases. You will not be allocated a place unless you are a single parent, have serious health problems, or live in other extremely difficult circum-stances. Day nurseries are usually open from 8.00 am until 6.00 pm, so if your child is eligible for a place you can work full- or part-time. Children are normally accepted on the recommendation of a social worker, but you yourself can make inquiries to your local social services department.

Private and workplace nurseries are few and far between. They are open for the full working day, but must be paid for. As they are often over-subscribed, they can charge what they wish, and the conditions they offer differ widely. No hard and fast advice can be given over the choice of a private nursery, except that you should spend some time there while it is in session so that you can judge the attitude of staff to the children and the amount of toys and activities provided. It is not always possible to assess a nursery by its accommodation. A scruffy church hall can house a lively and caring group, and a purpose-built centre can lack warmth. Many charities run nurseries which are usually good.

A childminder, almost always female, looks after children in her own home. Anyone can set up as a childminder, and because of this there have been dreadful stories of children being kept crowded and cooped up all day, with nothing provided for their interest and amusement. Recently, however, a lot of work has been done to improve this situation. Local councils have a system of registration for childminders who are considered to provide adequate care and facilities. Many also offer a support structure for their childminders in the form of centres and toy libraries where they can meet together and take the children in their care. The details of childcare are arranged privately between you and the childminder, but the latter should not look after more than three or four children (including any of her own) and should be willing to take them on outings and for any necessary visits to the clinic. Charges vary, but recently a minimum charge of £27 a week (or 80p an hour for part-time childminding) has been suggested by the National Childminders' Association. Your local social service department keeps a list of all registered childminders in the area.

A playgroup is not a great deal of help for working mothers but it may be useful if you wish to work irregularly, or for a very few hours each week. Playgroups are run all over the country, often in association with the Pre-School Playgroups Association. They are child-orientated in their aims and usually offer only half-day sessions. They accept children from the age of three and expect parents to participate in their running on a rota basis. If they fit your needs, they will certainly provide a happy environment for your child. A small charge is made for each session.

An alternative to playgroups, available in some parts of the country (mainly in the cities), are the nursery classes attached to some infants' schools. These also accept children from the age of three, usually for a morning or afternoon session. They are free, but are few and far between.

Employing a nanny is the surest way of ensuring your freedom to work, but it is expensive. Nannies either live in or come for specified hours each day. They should not be required to do general household duties, but most are happy to do light housework connected with the care of the children. The magazine *The Lady* is a good place to advertise for a nanny, and there are agencies in London and some of the larger provincial cities which specialise in matching nannies and employers.

The only other, cheaper way of ensuring individual care for your child while you work (unless you have an obliging relative living nearby) is to enter into a childshare arrangement with your children's father or a friend. This, quite simply, entails one partner looking after the children while the other works, and *vice versa*. Interaction, a community resource centre in North-West London, has a policy for employing parent-workers on this basis, but elsewhere it is something for which couples have to fight. When arranged between friends, it involves both partners finding jobs with compatible hours; if this proves possible it can work greatly to the benefit of both parents and children.

Childcare facilities for children who have started school are extremely difficult to find. This can pose real problems for you if your part-time hours are irregular or involve a reduced number of days each week, rather than a shortened working day. Some schools run late classes, or after-school play sessions, to help working parents, but the practice is by no means widespread. People who previously worked full-time, their preschool children having received full-time care, may find themselves changing to part-time work after the children start primary school because of the problems of after-school care.

There is one problem which both full-timers and part-timers come across and this is what to do with the children in the school holidays. In some larger cities holiday playschemes and workshops are organised, but there is little else available in the country as a whole. This situation probably pinpoints a difficulty felt by many mothers who work: it is the problem of guilt. However sure women are of their need and right to work, many still fear that their children will suffer through their absence. The equation seems quite simple: the longer the absence, the greater the guilt. Few women now believe that they should be available to their children at all times, but many feel happier if they have more involvement with their children than a full-time job allows. For this reason, you may decide to work part-time and achieve some balance between the conflicting responsibilities of home and work. But you may have to reckon with the costs of childcare which can be considerable, especially as a proportion of part-time pay. It is not (currently) possible to get tax relief on money spent in this way.

Care Facilities for Invalids and the Elderly

Because the numbers involved are far smaller, less attention has been paid to the plight of people who are prevented from working by the need to look after an invalid or elderly relative. Financial help is available, but there is no system of subsidised care that will give you the very basic freedom to work. Outside institutional care, there are only two forms of assistance, both organised locally by social services departments. These are home helps and geriatric visitors. Home helps are people who come into the homes of elderly or disabled people, to undertake household tasks they cannot do for themselves. In practice, they also perform a far more valuable function by providing support and companionship. Geriatric visitors help specifically with problems of the elderly. An additional form of support, particularly in rural areas, is the district nurse network which is run by the district health authority. The disadvantage of these forms of help is that they are available for only a short time each day, and therefore do not meet the needs of a person requiring constant attendance. The only way of providing complete care at home is to employ a companion/help yourself, and this is an option only open to the well-off.

This gap in our social provision is particularly cruel to people caught in its trap. Caring for an incapacitated person can be difficult and unrewarding, and the need for some relief away from the home can be intense. Beyond this, there is the problem of your own employment interests. You may not know how long a commitment to a relative will last, and if it ends when you are much above the age of 40 you could find it difficult to pick up the threads and find a job which suits your skills and experience. In most cases, it is advisable to work if you possibly can — and part-time work may be the most practicable solution.

Inquiries about care facilities can be made to your local social services department or to your family doctor.

Why Work?

On the face of it, the question 'Why work?' seems too obvious to be asked. You *know* why you want to work. The reasons may be various. You may need the money, or some relief from a solitary life at home; you may be attracted by the prospect of getting out a bit and meeting people; you may be looking to part-time work as a 'holding operation' on your career while your children are very young; you may need the satisfaction of working for its own sake; or you may be thinking of entering a new occupation or allowing yourself the time to build up a private interest. In all likelihood your reasons for wanting to work will influence you in your choice of job and the way in which you set about finding it.

But categories have an uncomfortable habit of overlapping, and jobs, particularly part-time jobs, of not being what they at first seemed. The single parent who seizes the most convenient job for the sake of the weekly pay packet may become increasingly bitter because his or her financial struggles are accentuated by the mundane nature of the work; the person who takes an unusual, but low-paid, job for its interest may end up resenting the small remuneration. It is sensible to look beyond your most immediate need and try to be as selective as circumstances permit.

Choosing a Job

Unfortunately, circumstances in the part-time job market militate against selectiveness, and though statistics indicate that your greatest chance of working in the future is to ensure that you are working in the present, acceptance of an inappropriate job *now* is unlikely to be in your interest in the long-term. Yet the pressures to accept unsuitable work may be enormous. Most part-time jobs occur in low-grade cleaning and catering work, and the 1982 National Training Survey revealed that one in 25 of part-timers with teaching qualifications, one in 12 part-timers with nursing qualifications, and one in six part-timers with clerical and commercial qualifications were working in low skilled catering and cleaning occupations in order to get hours that fitted their domestic responsibilities.

So, the first disadvantage of part-time working is the scarcity of suitable jobs in the right location offering convenient hours. It is easy, once the security and continuity of a full-time job have been abandoned, to find yourself in a downward spiral, taking work of increasingly lower status. And it can be difficult to escape. If you worked as a qualified secretary 10 years ago, it is difficult to convince an employer of your worth if your last job was as a hospital cleaner.

Many people accept low-grade work hoping that something more suitable might turn up, only to find that this never quite happens. Job-hunting, especially for the scarcer forms of part-time work, can be an occupation in itself. Few part-timers, as they operate a tight time-schedule, have the time or energy to job-hunt with any thoroughness. In this respect, once you commit yourself to a low-grade job, you reduce your chances of finding a more suitable one in the future. You should, if possible, decide upon the kind of work you want to do, bearing both the present and the future in mind. If you return, ultimately, to full-time working, your opportunities will be greater if you have maintained some links with the occupation of your choice, or that for which you were trained. Unless you are consciously seeking a change of occupation you should insist on working in your own field, but you must be prepared for the job to be of lower status than your last full-time post, as this is most commonly the case with part-time work.

Job Continuity

In Britain, the rewards for work are measured in terms of job continuity. Employment rights, social benefits and promotion opportunities are all linked to the length of continuous work. In this respect, part-timers are disadvantaged as they tend to stay in their jobs for shorter periods than full-timers. Even if you find, and keep, a suitable part-time job, you may find that you have sacrificed continuity in such matters as contributions to your pension scheme, and you will almost certainly be marking time, if not backsliding, in terms of promotion.

More drastic still, you may find yourself propelled into a pattern of frequent job changes. This can happen if you work for fewer than 16 hours a week and your employer decides to dispense with your services, or if you have no back-up to cope with crises in your family, or if you take on monotonous work which you cannot sustain for too long. And, once the pattern is established, you can be placed in a 'Catch 22' situation in which you are deprived of the means of staying in your job because you have not been in it long enough. You will not, for instance, be eligible for maternity leave, should you need it.

To maintain the advantages of job continuity throughout a period of part-time employment, you need an almost incredible combination of happy circumstances. You should remain in your chosen occupation, which must be one which makes provision for part-timers on the promotional ladder; your working hours must not fall below 16 a week; if you have babies you should space them at least two years apart so that you are eligible for maternity leave, and you should ensure that your domestic arrangements are foolproof at all times. Any childcare facilities you use must be adequate to deal with emergencies.

The chances are, however, that you have already sacrificed job continuity before you become a part-time worker.

The Career Break

Many part-timers are 'returners', that is, they have spent some years away from work while giving birth to their children. There is a tendency for younger women to return to work sooner than those aged over 35, but the practice of giving up work at the birth of the first child still persists. Most people who stop working remain at home until their families are complete, and therefore experience a significant interruption in their working lives.

Returning to work after such a break can be difficult. It takes time — not only to pick up the threads of the work you do, but to regain an image of yourself as a worker and feel sure of your identity and effectiveness. It is easy to lack confidence and feel humble, and the position assigned to you as a part-timer may not help you to combat this. On the other hand, part-time work may ease you gently back into work as well as being a practical necessity.

There is a strong argument for keeping in touch with both the habit and the practice of your work, even if it is only for a very few hours each week, or on an irregular basis, so that some degree of continuity is preserved. If you do not have the opportunity to do this, the next best thing is some kind of refresher course, taken on-the-job or before you resume work. Such courses are most likely to be available in female-dominated professions such as nursing, or those demanding very specific skills which are lost through lack of practice. In general, however, little attention is paid to the needs of women returning to work. At any event, it is sensible, when you are thinking of working again, to renew contacts with old colleagues, take a professional journal if this is appropriate, and generally acquaint yourself with what has been happening during your absence. Things can change alarmingly in only a few years, and it is misleading to believe that you will be able to pick up the threads where you left off, both smoothly and painlessly.

Re-training

Taking a complete break can, in some cases, be a positive benefit. Once outside the confines of your previous job you may feel that you would like to try something completely different. It is while they are away from work that some women, who left school with no qualifications, take a course of training which leads on to opportunities which would otherwise have been closed to them. There is a new consciousness of the need for mid-life education, particularly for women, and initiatives are being taken in setting up part-time courses, by adult education institutes, colleges of further education and poly-technics. Not all courses are specifically job-orientated, but attending any form of study is likely to widen your perspective and increase your confidence.

If you wish to test your ability to study, and you have young children, a good way to start is by attending the Pre-School Playgroups course. These courses take place on one day a week in a variety of locations all over the country. They are completely non-competitive; you will not be expected to take any exams; and the subject of study is the development of young children. A playgroup, and sometimes a creche, is available during the class, and students have the additional advantage of meeting others in a similar situation to their own.

Part-time training is as much an issue as part-time work, as it offers new opportunities which may offset the generally disadvantageous position in the job-market of people who have, for whatever reason, interrupted their working life. It is also a way of making a new start while keeping a hold on their present job, for people who would like to change their occupation. Not enough training for part-time work is yet available, but possible sources of information are listed in Part 3 of this book (see pp 184-6).

Job Satisfaction and the Marginality of Part-time Workers

It is almost impossible to separate job satisfaction from the question of 'marginality', as satisfaction derives from valuing, and being valued for, the work you do. Marginality is a term used to describe a state in which you are regarded as a sideline, rather than as a mainstream worker — a kind of 'extra' of whom less is expected and to whom less is offered. All part-time workers suffer from marginality to some extent and if it impinges too much on the day-to-day atmosphere in which your work is done, it may not be possible to achieve job satisfaction.

In general, marginality is felt most by people who work in a social context, because they are constantly aware of the distinctions drawn between themselves and full-timers. Marginality is felt least by those who work at home. They may be less favourably treated than full-timers, but they do not have the evidence of this around them. Across the board, part-timers are paid less than full-timers *pro rata*. Sometimes they are paid at a lower hourly rate; sometimes they work at jobs for which there are no full-time equivalents and which are held in low esteem; mostly, their lesser pay reflects their lack of perks. They may be excluded from production bonuses, overtime rates, paid holidays, and all those extras which boost the wages of their full-time colleagues.

Not all employers exclude part-timers from benefits on every count, though it is rare for any to give them complete parity with full-time workers. The John Lewis Partnership, for instance, admits *all* permanent employees to partnership, which is a profit sharing scheme, but part-timers who work less than a specified number of hours a week may be excluded from the pension scheme, membership of the residential club or discount. Many small employers are generous (though paternalistic) towards their part-timers, and are willing to be flexible over working hours. In general, part-timers can expect holiday pay but not inclusion in a company pension scheme. Neither can they expect overtime rates, as unsocial hours are often a feature of *normal* part-time shifts. However, whatever the position with regard to benefits, the main impediment to higher earnings is the lack of promotion. It is almost unknown, except in cleaning and catering jobs which are staffed mainly by part-timers, for part-time workers to be appointed to supervisory posts or grades reflecting responsibility.

This limitation works in two ways. You are denied status — and, if you previously held a responsible post, this may be hard to swallow — but you are also free of the many fringe duties which fall upon full-timers. Nobody will think to ask *you* to attend the lunch-time meeting, to organise the office party, or to undertake the many extra tasks which crop up in any workplace. You are a person who arrives at a certain time, does the work allotted to you, and then leaves. You are not generally expected to be involved in the general life of the workplace in the same way as a full-timer.

It is hard to evaluate the effect of these attitudes, but they will become apparent in many small ways and, according to your temperament and expectations, will add up to give you a feeling either of freedom, or of being an outsider — of being inessential apart from the routine work you do. You will see the life of the workplace going on around you, but you may find it difficult to feel you are a part of it. You will hear of events and crises which happened in your absence; your opinion on work matters will rarely be sought and the assumption will be that you have none to give. You will find yourself left out of the communication network. People will forget to tell you what has happened, simply because you were not around when it was being discussed. Events, special visits, and new initiatives, will take you unawares and, if you tax them with their silence, your colleagues will usually look incredulous and say, 'But I thought you knew!' There is usually no deliberate, or malicious, intention to exclude you. People may be friendly and welcoming, but will view you as a 'visiting' worker, rather than an essential part of the establishment.

The extent to which this situation affects the quality of your working life will depend partly upon the kind of work you do — partly upon your previous employment experience and partly upon your self-image and expectations of yourself as a worker. If you feel happier being organised by other people, or if you see yourself as an organiser of things rather than people, you will probably fare better than a person who previously was used to co-ordinating the work of others. Management of *people* is a role hardly ever allotted to part-timers. If your skills and experience fit the job, you will probably also find most satisfaction in work which can be broken down into self-contained units, because you will be able to feel responsible for a complete task or set of tasks. Many cleaners who feel responsible for their own territory achieve considerable involvement with their work, and people in a range of 'caring' jobs, which are easily split into 'caseloads', feel similarly rewarded. It is worth mentioning that jobs involving caring for others appear to offer high satisfaction for women returning to work even if they had previously worked in a different occupation. In these cases, job satisfaction can be more important than matters of status. Motherhood alters the perspectives of many people and can be the stimulus for rethinking and new goals. It is particularly ironical that it also reduces the opportunities available, as options for work and training are limited for the part-timer.

In-service Training

Many of the jobs undertaken by part-timers involve in-service training rather than prior qualifications. Even in work where initial training is a prerequisite, technical advances and changing work practices make in-service training important. Yet part-timers are often denied these opportunities altogether, or are offered an unsatisfactory second best.

When training is undertaken through a short course, part-timers are usually not allowed to go, or are not encouraged to think of themselves as candidates for 'improvement'. Even in work areas where part-time work is the norm, the hours of the course may be too long for a person with home commitments (see p 107). The commonest form of training takes place on-the-job and usually entails watching someone else doing the work and being given the benefit of a little time and explanation. In jobs where this is the case, part-timers are often employed at periods of peak activity when it is difficult for more experienced colleagues to give them adequate attention. They are often left to pick up their skills as best they can, and this can be a hair-raising experience. You may find yourself working at pressure, feeling very inadequate and ham-handed, and longing for the time to go through your routines slowly with some reassuring person to guide you.

An article in the *Training Officer Monthly* ('Part-timers also need training', A Mallier and M Rosser, June 1981) acknowledged this difficulty. The authors maintained that the training of part-time workers was inadequate, not only in terms of practical inefficiencies, but also in terms of content, as no differentiation was made between training given to full-timers and that given to part-timers. The assumption was that part-time staff are often engaged in a narrower range of tasks and therefore do not need the breadth of training given to a full-timer. It was admitted that this would limit their promotion prospects, but, nevertheless, in the deployment of part-timers a scaled-down form of training was suggested as the most effective. As long as such arguments are propounded in the pages of influential journals, there is little hope of reversing the thinking which relegates part-timers to a second-class position at work and must, in many cases, reduce the quality of their working lives.

Part-timers' Work Attitudes

There is a general admission from employers that part-timers are more productive, *pro rata*, than full-time workers. The assumption has been that they come fresh to the job and, as they work for fewer hours, have more energy to expend. A look at the hectic life of the average part-timer, who dashes from work to collect children from school and then home to fill the washing machine and cook the evening meal, would seem to question this assumption.

People who are happy at work work harder, and it may be that the sociability of the workplace enhances even the most routine job when the alternative is isolation in the home. Sociability was mentioned as a motivation by several people who recounted their experiences, and those who sought it usually found their jobs rewarding. There is ample evidence that people are able to sustain tedious work well below their levels of competence, and the part-time shifts during which such work is often done are said to be characterised by good humour and friendliness. The desire for the particular companionship of working alongside others is obviously strong.

It may also be that people in satisfying part-time posts value the stimulation of work more highly than full-timers, who take it for granted. But it is distinctly possible that many part-timers feel less secure, less valued as employees, than their full-time colleagues, and therefore more determined to justify themselves through their work performance. Lack of acknowledgement was mentioned several times in the case studies, but the people complaining of it did not claim that they worked less hard as a result. Many, it seemed, worked harder. There was a tendency for employers to take advantage of hard-working part-timers, especially in offices. Several people considered that they were expected to get through more work, proportionate to their hours, than full-timers, and to stay beyond their leaving time if, for instance, presented with a letter to be typed five minutes before they were due to go.

Conversely, part-timers themselves find it difficult to 'fiddle' their hours to their own advantage, as their arrival and departure at different times from the rest of the workforce is a well-witnessed event. This applies to people working a shorter day. Those on a reduced number of full days are less likely to be affected by such attitudes. Where mention was made of a desire to 'fiddle' hours, this was always in connection with personal difficulties — mainly those pertaining to children. It reflected the need for more flexibility, rather than the wish to cheat employers of their scheduled hours of work. Part-timers as a whole emerged as a conscientious group, who sought the same kinds of satisfactions as any other workers, not least the satisfaction of doing the job well. They did not appear to seek to make, or, indeed, make a second-class contribution to their work, and most accepted their second-class status with remarkable equanimity.

Career Patterns

The low status of part-time jobs most acutely affects those people who aspire to a 'career' and who may already have set their foot upon the promotional ladder. Most career structures in Britain today are very rigid. They are seen in terms of continuity and people are expected to rise through them in a set order and at a certain pace. Few allowances are made for divergences from the normal pattern, and people who depart from this put themselves at great disadvantage. A few professions have been forced, by the need to retain the services of skilled staff, to create part-time posts of graduated responsibility, but most make no provision for part-timers in their promotional structure. In most cases, therefore, part-time working can be seen, at best, as a holding operation; at worst it can be seen as an acknowledgement that personal circumstances have put you outside the promotional stakes. And, once you relinquish your full-time post for an 'ungraded' part-time one, there is no guarantee that you will be able to start again from where you left off when you are ready to resume full-time working. Past achievements are soon forgotten and part-timing carries its own identity.

There is no intrinsic reason, relating to the contribution part-timers could make, why this should be so. Where part-timers themselves set the employment structure it is a very different story, as an employment agency called Part Time Careers demonstrates.

Part Time Careers deals solely with placing people in part-time posts. The jobs it offers are office vacancies in central London and include secretarial posts, administrative work and accountancy and bookkeeping positions. It is a commercial organisation and was founded by Kay Sykes in 1974 in the belief that employers had a need of the expertise of people who, for one reason or another, had been lost to full-time work. The business expanded rapidly, and today five people are employed, of whom only the managing director works full-time. The success of the company demonstrates both the need for, and the effectiveness of part-time working at all levels of responsibility.

The chances are, however, that you will not be fortunate enough to find such an escape from prevailing attitudes and limitations, but will be left to make your personal adjustment to the more usual situation that obtains. For most people, part-time working is a compromise, and probably the most overwhelming argument you will find in its favour is the need which prompted you to consider it in the first place.

Part 2

Introduction

Part 2 of this book sets out to be informative about a wide range of part-time occupations, but it is not a careers manual. No information is given about career structures or training requirements *per se* as this seems inappropriate for two reasons. First, it is unusual for young people to begin their working lives in part-time posts so it is reasonable to assume that the reader already has some knowledge of his or her line of work. Second, part-time workers are almost always outside the career structure for their occupational group in that their chances of promotion are nil or minimal.

The following chapters are written in the spirit of an inquiry, supported by relevant information, which seeks to answer the two questions: 'What is it like to work part time?' and 'What might part-timing be like for me?' The main opportunities available to part-timers are outlined and an attempt is made to describe the situation people will find in occupations with which they may already be familiar working full-time. Mention is made of part-time training courses or training which is geared to re-entry to a known occupation as this is clearly relevant. In occupations in which practice is constantly changing, or skills need to be maintained, 're-orientation' courses are sometimes run for people returning to work, and these are discussed in the appropriate chapters. On the education front, an acknowledgement of the need, particularly among women, for mid-life training has led to the growth of 'Access' courses, many of which are part-time. They are listed in 'A Survey of "Access" Courses in England', edited by Susan Lucas and Peter Ward, which is available from the School of Education, University of Lancaster, Lancaster LA1 4YW.

The fewer hours and diminished involvement which may result from working part-time can turn a previously harassed scene into a pleasantly stimulating interlude, or reduce job satisfaction to a disastrous degree and induce a feeling of marginality. Which of these two extremes is the case (and there are, of course, many intermediate positions) will depend as much upon the personality of the part-timer and the peripheral conditions of work as on the essential nature of the occupation. Attention is therefore given to factors such as attitudes of employers and colleagues, convenience, and job-satisfaction, rather than to detailed accounts of the jobs themselves, of which the reader may already be aware.

The backbone of the inquiry is the personal experience of 32 part-timers who described their jobs, their circumstances and their reactions to the situations in which they found themselves. They were chosen at random for their availability, their willingness to help, and because their jobs were representative of a wide range of part-time occupations. Women with young children predominated (26), five being single parents. One interviewee was easing off her working life with retirement in mind, and with the additional motivation of spending more time on interests beyond her paid work. Only one interviewee was a man and no one was disabled — regrettably, as the disabled comprise a small, but significant, category of part-time workers.

No one interviewed held a management position; one community worker worked in a co-operative and therefore shared in the management of the project, but it proved impossible to find any one with a management role in a more conventional sense, even in the realm of job-sharing. Apparently, employers do not yet acknowledge that managerial duties can be undertaken part-time. There was, among the employees too, a fairly general acceptance that part-timers cannot expect to be supervisors, though some people found this limitation frustrating.

Each interviewee completed a short questionnaire from which the above facts (and more) were obtained (see Appendix C, p 178) but the interviews themselves were intentionally unstructured to encourage a subjective response. The aim was to collect together a variety of personal experiences, in which people talked about matters which most affected them rather than replying to a set line of inquiry. In this way it was hoped that many points would arise which would be valuable for the reader either because of the frequency of their repetition or because of their relevance to the reader's own situation.

Chapter 5
Domestic and Catering Work

Introduction

Scrubbing a floor or slaving over a hot stove may not be everybody's idea of bliss, but few jobs in domestic and catering solely comprise these activities. There are good and bad jobs in this field, and the best have a lot to recommend them.

Job availability is good: because of the widespread need for this type of work, jobs are available almost everywhere, except in the most rural areas.

Apart from a few positions which involve cooking, no previous qualifications or experience are needed for jobs of this nature, though certain personal qualities may be preferable to others. As a large proportion of jobs in domestic and catering work are part-time there are more opportunities for supervisory positions than in other part-time occupations. There is also a wide choice in hours of work.

To offset these advantages, most of the jobs carry a low status and the work is often hard. Pay is poor — from about £1.80 an hour (in 1986), unless you are a supervisor or are fortunate enough to have a generous private employer. There were people who remained unsympathetic to the hospital workers when they took industrial action in 1982 because, they argued, take-home pay was more than the amounts claimed in the press. This was *not* true for part-timers in this field. Full-timers can increase their earnings by working overtime, but this is not an option open to part-timers. Usually, there is a ruling that no worker who works less than, say, 30 hours is eligible for extra payment for unsocial hours, and if part-timers do work unsocial hours it is assumed that they will have elected to work these hours as part of a *normal* part-time shift. In addition, most part-timers are limited by their personal circumstances. They have no more time available which they can use for paid work. As a part-timer, therefore, you will be paid the basic hourly rate and no more.

Finding a Job

The large, well-known employers (chain stores, hospitals, local councils, schools etc) seldom advertise their vacancies as they can usually fill them with people who inquire personally. So there may be no alternative to a round of personal visits, and this can be depressing if you do not soon meet with success. However, smaller firms often advertise in the local press or use Jobcentres. (For information about Jobcentres, see Part 3, p 181.) Some jobs appear among the notices in newsagents' shop windows, and if you want to work privately it is worth while advertising *your* services in this way. Working for an agency can lead to permanent employment. Look them up in the Yellow Pages under 'Employment Agencies' or 'Domestic Cleaning'.

Probably the best all-round method of job-hunting is to ask around your friends, especially those who have the kinds of jobs you might like to do. Many schools first offer vacancies to the parents of their pupils, so it is worth while making your interest known to the staff.

Domestic Work

All buildings, from factories and large institutions to your own and your neighbours' houses, need to be cleaned. This gives you some idea of the extent and range of jobs available. With such a wide choice, you will need to decide what kind of cleaning you are willing to do.

Cleaning in factories, hospitals, pubs and large offices is hard work, whereas cleaning shops and private houses is a great deal easier. Schools and colleges vary, according to the part of the building you are required to clean.

It is rare for cleaners to work alone, unless they work in very small premises, and the sociability of working in a team is one of the attractions of the job for many people. There is another factor which will influence the nature of your job. This is whether the cleaning is done while the building is functioning, or while it is shut to everyone except the team of cleaners. In most cases cleaning is more conveniently done while the building is empty, but some premises function around the clock and in these, cleaning must be carried out alongside the other activities. This happens in hospitals, residential homes, hotels and private houses.

If you are a no-nonsense person, who likes to get on with the job without interference or hindrance, you will probably be happier in an empty building. But there can be disadvantages, especially if you are cleaning up after individuals rather than in anonymous public areas. Your annoyance with the man who leaves his tea bags in the ash tray and his orange peel on the floor may build up to alarming proportions because you never see him to tell him how you feel. This is a hazard, particularly with office cleaning, which incidentally was mentioned by more than one of the interviewees as the most unrewarding and hardest work they had ever done. The fact that you will never get recognition and thanks for what you do except, perhaps, from your supervisor, is also one which you should not underestimate.

If, on the other hand, you work alongside the normal functioning of the premises, you may find that people get in your way but you will, to an extent, become involved in the everyday life of the place. This can add to the interest of the job, and, when your presence gives companionship to the lonely or ill, can be very rewarding.

Work Routines and Hours of Work

You will usually have some routines that you are required to carry out, but as long as your work is up to standard the way you go about it will normally be up to you. Even in large establishments you will be allotted your own 'territory', so you will probably feel some responsibility and satisfaction in the work you do.

The commonest work shifts are in the early morning or evening (6.00 − 9.00 am and 6.00 − 9.00 pm). People who do not wish to work during these evening hours may find an alternative in schools, where shifts begin when the children go home and last until about 6.00 pm. In between these hours are daytime shifts which will alter according to the needs of each establishment. If you do private or agency cleaning (see pp 96 - 97), you will be able to determine your hours by arrangement.

Terms of Employment

Your terms of employment will vary according to who you work for. In general, these are much improved since the days of the 1960s when May Hobbs led the fight for the unionisation of London's office cleaners.

If you work in the public sector, your pay and conditions will be clearly defined and you can expect to receive sick pay and paid holidays in relation to your length of service. An exception to this is the situation in schools and colleges where, because of the long holidays, there are rather different arrangements.

If you work for a private employer, your terms of employment are less certain. Under law you do not, as a part-timer, qualify for paid holidays as a statutory right. And you will not qualify for statutory sick pay unless your earnings are above the National Insurance threshold (£38.00 a week in 1986).

Cleaners, as a whole, are most unlikely to be included in an occupational pension scheme, though there may be some chance of this if you are employed in a supervisory post in the public sector.

One difficulty, if you work for a small employer, may be in finding out what your terms of employment actually are. In your own interests you should inquire what your position will be *before* you start work, as this is the time when the situation might be changed. For the kinds of questions you should ask, see Chapter 2 on contracts of employment (p 43).

There are so many settings in which cleaning is done that it would be impossible to describe them all. The following three examples have been chosen because they are forms of work which are available almost anywhere and are not restricted, like shop and office cleaning, to urban areas.

Hospital Cleaning
There are certain facts about hospital cleaning that you must be able to accept. You must not be too squeamish because you may have to deal with soiled dressings and other unpleasant products of illness. Hygiene is particularly important in hospitals and you will find your work governed by strict rules which require you to clean more extensively and thoroughly than you would in other settings. You will, for instance, clean at high levels, paying attention to curtain rails, ledges and pipes. You will also wash walls and disinfect lavatories and washing and waste disposal areas.

Hospitals generate feelings of loyalty and sociability among their staff. This is probably because hospital work, at all levels, is hard and often emotionally demanding, and this draws people together. Cleaning in a hospital can be a rewarding job, therefore, if you appreciate the friendliness of working companionship.

If you clean in outpatient clinics and administrative offices, your work will usually be done during an evening shift while the premises are empty. If you have a responsibility for in-patient areas, you will work a daytime shift; on the wards your work will be done around the patients. This can be particularly rewarding in mental, geriatric and other long-stay hospitals, because you will get to know the patients well and they may rely on you for help and companionship. Many cleaners in this situation feel that they perform a far more valuable service in this way than through the cleaning they do.

Most hospitals have a domestic department which is organised to suit the particular situation. In smaller hospitals, all the domestic staff may be part-timers, and supervisory positions will therefore be available on a part-time basis. In large hospitals the likelihood is that full-timers will be appointed to these positions.

Of course, the recent trend towards privatisation of hospital cleaning is undoubtedly leading to worsening terms and conditions of employment for employees, whether part-time or full-time.

Being a Home Help

Home helps are among the better paid domestic workers. This is because the job carries considerable responsibility beyond the strictly defined duties of domestic work.

Home helps are employed by the social services departments of local councils to help people who cannot manage by themselves. They visit their clients (as the people needing help are known) in their own homes and help out in whatever ways seem most necessary. Most clients are elderly and housebound, but a few may be disabled, recovering from hospitalisation, or families going through a difficult time.

The first duty of the home help is to respond to the wishes of the client and do whatever is required. This may be cleaning, shopping, getting a meal, going to the launderette or taking children to school. Sometimes there are unpleasant tasks to be done. You may have to empty commodes or deal with soiled bedding, but if you do tasks of this kind you are usually paid an additional allowance.

Occasionally, there may be situations in which it is necessary for you to decide how best you can help. This is because another important function of a home help is to be a link between the client and other helping agencies. You should be able to judge if a person is ill and needs to see a doctor; if a mother is undergoing such stress that the children are at risk; or if an elderly person needs more help than you can give. And if one day a door remains unanswered, you are the person on the spot to alert the authorities to the possibility that something is wrong. Also, particularly important, you may be the only visitor to save your client from unbearable loneliness — many elderly people, especially in cities, lead very isolated lives.

The hours which you work will usually be very flexible. In most areas there are two options: a morning shift from about 9.30 until 2.30, and an all-day shift starting at the same time and finishing about 4.30. You will have a 'caseload' of a certain number of clients, with time allowed for travelling between their homes. You will not be required to work every day of the week if you do not wish to, though you may be paid a small bonus if you do so. Work at weekends and on bank holidays is optional, and paid for at higher rates. However, you will have to make a regular commitment, and this means that you must work during school holidays. You will be on probation for the first six months and after this, if your work is satisfactory, your appointment will be permanent and you will be entitled to paid holidays and generous sick leave.

You will not need any qualifications or prior experience to become a home help, though you may be capable of doing practical tasks and have a sympathy with people, especially the elderly. Some authorities run induction courses for their home helps, and people who have taken them say that they have found them helpful in providing a broad idea of the job and thereby making it more satisfying.

Cleaning in Private Houses and Agency Cleaning
There are two ways of working as a cleaner in private houses: you can make a private arrangement or you can find work through an agency.

If you are able to make the contact yourself, privately arranged cleaning can be a convenient form of work. It is usually close to home; you can, within reason, state your own hours; and it may sometimes be possible to take a young child if this does not cause problems. Also, the work is usually fairly light and, once you know what your employer wants, it should be easy to get into a pleasant rhythm of work.

A lot will depend on how well you get on with your employer so it is a good idea to start on a trial basis for the first few weeks. It is also best to be clear from the outset about what each of you expects. In this form of employment you cannot expect the benefits a larger employer might give, such as sick leave or paid holidays. You will usually be paid only for the work you do, for as long as your services are required. In this sense, private cleaning is a form of freelancing.

If you do not wish to undertake these arrangements for yourself, you can work for an agency. Domestic agencies are to be found in most towns of any size and they send out cleaners on request. Usually there is a set charge, and you give to the agency a percentage of what you are paid.

One disadvantage of agency work is the lack of continuity, though this can be a source of interest as you see many different kinds of homes — and their occupants! Working this way will involve travelling, which may be difficult for you, but usually your expenses are paid. The other snag is that people tend to use agencies in an emergency, so you may find yourself required to do heavy spring-cleaning or to clear up after builders and decorators. Often, however, people contact an agency simply because they have been unable to find a regular cleaner, and in these cases, if the arrangement suits you both, there is nothing to stop you continuing it on a private basis.

Agency cleaning is often done by men, and it is convenient for students as you can work irregularly at hours to suit yourself.

Heavier forms of cleaning are available through agencies — anything from cleaning factories to giving a facelift to carpets in some palatial hotel. To do this specialised work, you must be prepared to wield heavy machinery.

CASE STUDIES

Marjorie. A Hospital Cleaner
Marjorie has three children, and only the youngest is still at school.

> 'I've always had work when I wanted it. I've never had unemployment money since coming to this country. I work evenings now, in a hospital, cleaning the clinics, from 6.00 until 9.00 pm, and I've been doing it for three years. It suits me, but I wouldn't mind something during the day too, now that my children are growing up. But I can't get my nerve up yet. I've been home for too long and you get into a rut.

I would be glad of more money but I don't want to work full-time. I could get this at the hospital from 7.30 am until 4.00 pm, but I don't want that. No matter what some people say, it's too much. And you don't get that much more money either. I get the same hourly rate as full-timers and the same holidays and sick pay, so that's not too bad.

At the hospital, everybody likes to stay in their own jobs. We each have our own clinics and we know what to do. If I go on holiday they can send anybody, and often they don't mind how they do it. But I mind — when I get back the clinic is in a terrible state and I have to start all over again from scratch.

It's different from other cleaning. Some of the places are really filthy, especially the dental clinics. Some people get pricked with needles in the rubbish — you can pick up anything. But the atmosphere is pleasant, and if we finish early we sit around and have a good old gossip. You get paid less than in other places, of course. There's a supervisor to every unit, but I don't think a part-timer could get to that. I don't think they'd like it at all!

My husband gets paid once a month, so I need my weekly money for the shopping. And being at home all day, I can do all the cooking then and feed everybody before I leave. I don't have to travel far either. I know a woman who has to travel one hour to her job and I wouldn't like that. I like to work close to home'.

Yvonne. Domestic Supervisor in a Psychiatric Hospital

The cleaning of this hospital is carried out by two teams of part-time workers, one working from 8.30 am to 1.30 pm, and the other in the evenings from 6.00 to 9.00 pm. Both combine to work alternate weekends. Yvonne is the supervisor of the morning shift.

'I have never worked full-time. My parents were both invalids and I looked after them before and after I was married. Finally, they died within a year of each other. My children were all at school and I thought I was in danger of going round the bend. My husband suggested that I should find a job and I saw this one advertised in the local paper.

That was 13 years ago, and the hospital was setting up a new domestic department. Previously, the work had been done by ward orderlies and the patients helped too — without pay, of course! At first, I was in charge of seven workers. Now there are over 30, including two male ex-patients who have the only full-time jobs. It's not so much a case of the hospital growing as of the patients being given better conditions.

At first it was strange just to leave home and come here. And I had to get used to telling people what to do. I think it took me about six months to get settled in. I am responsible to the domestic manager and it is my job to see that the cleaners do their work. I tell them where to go, and if we have anybody away I organise the women so that all the work gets done. We like to keep them on their own wards as far as possible, but when we are short they have to help out.

Once a fortnight I do a quality check on the wards and if I see anybody doing anything I don't like, I will show them how to do it.

I also insist on doing some of the long-term jobs, like sealing floors, myself, as I know how I want it done. But otherwise, I don't do any of the cleaning. To be a good supervisor you have to be able to move your staff around and get *them* to do the work.

As a supervisor, you are the person in the middle. You get some bad-tempered women who don't like being moved, and you get the hassle from both sides. You've got to keep your staff happy and not be on at them all the time if they are to do a decent job. I am friendly with all, but not with any particular one. The job commands quite a bit of respect. Even the nurses say, 'Watch out! Here's Mrs F coming'!'

Mary. Cleaner in the same hospital

Mary has seven children, most of them now grown up. Like Yvonne, she has worked at the hospital for 13 years.

'Before I was married I did nursing, but afterwards I wanted part-time work because the hours were better for my children. My husband was disabled during the war and could only get a low-paid job, so I had to help fill the family coffers, so to speak. I found that the hours I had to work nursing did not fit in, so I started doing contract cleaning.

When I first came here my youngest child was a baby, so I took the evening shift and I've stayed on it ever since. My husband came home at 5.00 pm and I caught the bus at the corner at 5.15. It has been difficult at times. Two of my children are delicate and, during illness, they have had to come first although I feel committed to my job. But we managed.

I work on a bad spastics ward, and when I first saw the patients I thought I couldn't take it — I thought I'd be handing in my notice at the end of the week. Some of them looked so grotesque. But those you think you are not going to like turn out to be your favourites. Now, I am very attached to them and they depend on me, too. You come to think of the patients as your own children and want to help in any way you can. Although most of them can't talk, they understand, and they like you to bring things for them. When I come back from holiday, they all want a cuddle. That's what makes the job. I shouldn't like to be cleaning empty rooms.

My son is doing psychiatric nursing, and my youngest daughter, who is still at school, comes here with me at weekends. She loves the children and wants to be a nurse too. Maybe I have influenced them.

I don't want to work full-time because I am still much needed at home. Also, I like to write. I have written a story — a romantic one with a Romany background, because my husband is of Romany descent — and I am writing another one now. I am also doing a family tree and I've gone back to 1829 so far.

This job is ideal. I love it! The only disadvantage is the other workers. Being all women together, they tend to get bitchy at times, usually about little things that don't matter. If I could just get on with the job it would be perfect.'

Carol. Home Help

Carol works in an inner city area, weekdays from 9.00 am until 2.00 pm. She has three children aged 10, 8 and 4 and has been a home help for four months.

'This is my first job for some time, apart from doing some typing for my father-in-law. I wanted to wait until the children were older and I felt I could cope without skimping on my work or disrupting the family. It has turned out very well. The hours suit me and nobody seems to have suffered, though I do find that I am busier than I used to be. I used to spend time at the children's school, hearing children read and helping with art. I can't do that any more.

I knew a bit about home helps before I decided to become one, because I have a friend who is a supervisor. I work the morning shift on every weekday, but I don't work weekends or bank holidays. I've had quite a bit to do with old people and I like them. Most of my clients are elderly and I find I get along with them. You have to be understanding. Your attitude is the most important thing about the job.

On my first day the supervisor came out with me, but after that I was on my own. I visit four clients every day and I find that I am not rushed. I can afford the time to do any little extras they want. Some never do anything for themselves and others only want the carpet swept because they can't bend. You get good and bad. I have to empty commodes, but apart from that I haven't had any really nasty jobs yet. We encourage the old people to do what they can for themselves, and we always ask what *they* want us to do rather than coming in and deciding for ourselves because, after all, it is their home.

Mostly I visit the same people so I get to know them well. I have two I go to every day, and others I visit twice a week. One old lady has bad breathing in the morning so I go in early and 'do' for her then, because· later in the day she can manage for herself. I always give her breakfast so that I know she has had it. Eating can be a problem with some old people. If they live alone, they sometimes don't bother.

I think your job can depend on the area you are in. In some places, people can be very snooty — elderly people particularly — and treat you like a servant. But here, I find that the clients are really grateful for what I do. I enjoy the work a lot. You don't have anyone breathing down your neck and you meet a great variety of people. But I think you must want to work in this way, and not just do it for the money although it is good.

When I left school, I worked as bank clerk and then as an administrator for an American firm which had a computerised system for hotel reservations. That was interesting, but I don't think I would go back to it now. Perhaps when the children are older I might go back into an office — maybe in a social services department. I think you change after having children. You have a broader outlook. When you are single, everything revolves around *you*.'

Catering

The catering industry is characterised by lack of organisation and diversity. Employers range from large public institutions to small restaurants employing only a handful of people. A large proportion of catering workers — something approaching 40 per cent — work part-time, because part-timers suit the needs of the industry and the jobs are often convenient for them.

Work Tasks and Hours of Work
Work in catering can be divided into two groups: behind the scenes and 'out front'. In the kitchens, most part-timers are employed as kitchen assistants, engaged mainly on vegetable preparation or washing up. In restaurants, part-timers are not usually employed as cooks, though in schools and workplace catering they may be. Some training is needed to work as a cook. This is sometimes available through your employer.

In the restaurant or dining room, part-timers are employed as waiters and waitresses, or as cafeteria hands, serving behind the counter or clearing the tables. The skills needed for these tasks can be learnt on-the-job. Bar work in a pub is demanding as you have to learn all the different drinks and how to serve them. It can also be extremely busy and sometimes exhausting.

Because catering work is geared to the times at which people eat, much of it involves working unsocial hours, in the evenings — and this can mean *late* evening — and at weekends. There are opportunities for daytime work, however, notably in schools and in workplace catering, if the main provision is the midday meal. In other places, such as hospitals, which cater around the clock, a variety of shifts will be available.

Working Conditions
Conditions generally can be difficult. Working in a hot, steamy kitchen is not for everybody and you can feel rushed off your feet. This applies to waiting as well. It is not safe to judge conditions by the outward face or 'class' of the establishment because some of the large, smart hotels have, in the past, been the worst employers and this is possibly the case today. You may be better off working for one of the 'hamburger and chip' chain companies, where work routines are usually well organised and simplified by using convenience foods. On the whole, working in the public sector will probably give you the best chance of working under reasonable conditions, though the pay may be less than you could get elsewhere. The education and health services are the largest public employers of catering workers.

Terms of Employment

A survey of part-time workers (Hurstfield, 1978) found that catering workers were the most disadvantaged group in many ways. They were the least likely to be covered by an employer's sick pay scheme and only 50 per cent received paid holidays. Statistics for those receiving benefits are probably inaccurate, owing to the fact that many catering workers are employed on a casual basis. Working on a casual basis need not affect the quality of the job while you are actually doing it (see the case study on page 104) but it will leave you with no protection, either to retain your work on a regular basis or to cope with personal emergencies which might arise.

The public sector will offer you the most clearly defined and standardised terms of employment; those offered by private employers will vary tremendously. The best can be very generous; the worst, appalling. Many catering workers are covered by Wages Councils, so they should be guaranteed a minimum wage and, sometimes, certain other agreed benefits. Workers in hostels and unlicensed hotels, however, are outside the Wages Council structure, and unless they have a trade union to promote their interests (and they rarely do) they are in a poor position.

Catering workers in small restaurants are particularly vulnerable to exploitation. On the whole you will be better off as part of a medium-sized or large establishment, even if the catering section is small.

It would be hard to find a greater variety of jobs and working situations in any other occupation than can be found in catering. The jobs described below have been chosen for the following reasons: all illustrate the happier side of catering; two are forms of work which are often readily available; one offers a promotion structure within the context of part-time work — a rare opportunity; and one shows how chance (if you are lucky enough to find and then respond to it) can land you with a job which is both more demanding and rewarding than is usually the case.

Workplace Catering

This is a form of catering not generally known about because the general public does not have access to it. It is, however, quite extensive as many firms provide eating facilities for their employees. The catering may range from canteen and cafeteria provision to prestige dining, though the former is probably more common. The great advantage of workplace catering is that there is little or no commercial motive for providing the service, and terms of employment (including pay) may therefore be more generous than the norm. Another favourable aspect of this work is that catering is often restricted mainly to the midday meal, so working hours will be daytime ones where this is the case.

Waiting

The amount of waiting available has been restricted by the growth of the cafeteria system, but this has not affected the more up-market eating places and plenty of jobs are to be found.

Waiting, of all the jobs in catering, sets the tone of the establishment and, in the smartest restaurants, is conducted rather like a pageant, carefully timed and orchestrated by the head waiter. Wherever you work, you must be neat and presentable and look calm but efficient, whatever mood is prevailing in the kitchen. If you take customers' orders, you will find many people hesitant and seemingly bent on getting you in a muddle, but you have to accept it all with a smile! You need to know how to serve the various foods on offer, but you can learn this on-the-job. In waiting, watch and then do is the rule.

The aristocracy of waiters are the head waiters, and part-timers will not be considered for these posts. Otherwise, wine waiting is thought to be the best job. It demands a knowledge of wines and a certain style in serving them, and usually commands the highest tips. Wine waiters or waitresses, however, work extremely late hours.

Wages for waiting are often low, based on the assumption that they will be boosted by tips. Tips can mount up, but not always for part-timers. If they are pooled and then shared out, you may miss your share if you are not on the spot at the right time. You will rarely receive tips if you wait at special functions because the bill is not usually paid at the time of the function. Even if a gratuity is added, it seldom finds its way back to the waiters and waitresses.

Working in the School Meals Service

Despite the derogatory jokes children love to make about school dinners, considerable organisation and thought go into producing them. Each local education authority has a central training and advisory/supervisory department to maintain standards, and appointments to this service are usually full-time. In the schools themselves, however, part-time work is available and there are opportunities to rise from kitchen assistant to cook. Cook supervisors, however, usually work full-time.

Part-timing in school kitchens is a most convenient form of work as it occupies school hours only, gives you the school holidays off work, and is often available locally. There are two main levels of responsibility: kitchen assistant and cook. You can work as a kitchen assistant without previous training and experience, but you will usually need qualifications to work as a cook. Most authorities have their own system of on-the-job training for cooks but this includes attendance at training centres which may not be convenient for everybody.

Pay is around £2.50 an hour for kitchen assistants and more for cooks. General terms of employment are fair, and the main disadvantage concerns pay during the school holidays. Arrangements vary from one authority to another, but you cannot expect full pay for the holiday periods. At most, you will receive a retainer during these weeks. This considerably reduces the overall income and probably makes this work unsuitable for people who have no additional source of income.

CASE STUDIES

Mary. Workplace Catering Supervisor

Mary trained as a receptionist. She has three children aged 13, 10 and 8 and, while they were very young, did a variety of agency jobs. She has held her present post for six years and has sole responsibility for catering for a firm of solicitors.

'I had no training for catering, and when I took the job it was for a three months' trial period. I was unsure about it myself, but I was desperate for a week's work so I took it. Once I had started, it was like a dream. I'd always done this work at home and it was something I felt happy doing. I found the job through an agency I had been working for as a 'temp'. The firm really wanted a full-timer, but I couldn't do that so I promised them I would get the work done in less time — and I did!

Officially, I work from 10.30 am until 3.30 pm, but I can be flexible as long as the job gets done. I cook a three-course lunch for the partners and their clients and I'm responsible for everything from shopping to clearing away before I leave. The numbers I cater for can be anything from nine to 18.

I never plan in advance. I have a half-hour journey and usually I decide while I'm on the tube what I will cook. I've got my routine well organised, otherwise I wouldn't get everything done in the time. Also, I'm a quick worker. I drop the children at school at 9.15 and I'm in work by 10 o'clock. I serve the partners coffee and clear away by 10.45; then I get money from the cashier — there are no limits. I take what I need — and do the shopping for lunch. By 11.45 I am cooking, and I lay up and serve the meal for 1.00 pm.

I'm the one who waits at table and sometimes I have people in the dining room *and* a special boardroom lunch. I do anything they ask, even special diets for foreign visitors, and they know they can rely on me to produce a meal at the shortest notice. When I've cleared away, I am free to go home.

Since I took the job I've gone to night school for a Cordon Bleu course, paid for by my employers, but I don't think I benefited. We all like good food in our family and I am experimental. I can work from books. So I think that most of what I know I taught myself. I had to learn about wines, too, and build up a basic stock. I was able to plan the kitchen as I wanted it with all the labour-saving devices and a microwave oven to help me keep up my speed. My employers are very good to me. I get a good salary, sick pay, luncheon vouchers and five weeks' paid holiday. But, in return, they know I'll work hard.

It is a very sociable job and I love it. I know all the partners well, and who enjoys his food. I will make a special effort for them. And on off-days, I can always plan something easier. School holidays and emergencies with the children are no problem as I have my mother living with us. The main disadvantage is having to look good every day. I am on show and I don't feel that I can wear trousers or be too casual. But it is worth it to have a job where time flies. In so many other jobs I was always watching the clock.'

Peggy. Waitress

Peggy has five children whose ages range from 13 to 27. She has been a member of a waitress circle, waiting at special functions, for 20 years. Officially, the work is done on a casual basis but, as she explains, it can be a reliable and continuing source of income.

'To get into waiting at special functions — banquets as they are called — you need a friend to introduce you, but once you are inside the circle you can usually get all the work you want. The person who first employs you will ask what hours you are free, whether evenings or lunch-times, weekdays or weekends, and will ring you when work is available at suitable times. They never know from week to week, as bookings are often made only a week in advance, but this can be an advantage as you are free to say 'no' if you have a child ill or have planned something else.

I found that local firms would ask each other for contacts, so once you are 'in' with one employer you are likely to be offered work by others. I started off with a fairly up-market employer and I think we were well thought-of by others, so that might have helped to increase my offers of work.

When you start, you get yourself kitted up with the right clothes — something black or navy, and a small white apron — and present yourself along with the others. You take your orders from the head waiter or waitress, who controls the timing of everything. Usually, you begin by preparing your serving cloth and spoons and, perhaps, the coffee things as well. Sometimes you will be asked to lay up the tables. Then you wait behind the scenes until the serving begins. Most newcomers are given vegetables to serve. This is the easiest and you can copy what the others do. It is up to you to show that you can learn the work. If you don't you won't be asked again! But, on the whole, food at banquets is quite ordinary and you don't get faced with strange dishes you don't know what to do with.

After the meal has been served the waitresses have their own meal — usually the same as the guests — and can linger over it during the coffee, speeches and so on. The time this takes varies, but it can be quite long and it makes the work very sociable. I know that a lot of my friends who are at home all day with young children do the work as much for its sociability as for the money.

When the guests have gone you clear away. I have never been asked to wash up. The most I have done is to rinse the glasses or the plates, ready for the dishwasher. But usually it is enough to stack the dirty things away for the kitchen staff.

You are paid at the end of each function. Pay varies from one employer to another, but it will always be for between three and five hours' work. Tax can be a problem, especially if you work for more than one employer. It is left up to you and it can be hard to decide when to begin paying it. I started paying when I had built up a regular two nights a week. If you are well-paid I think you can afford to pay tax, but with a low-paying employer it would scarcely be worth the trouble working.'

Pat. School Kitchen Assistant

Pat has two children aged 6 and 8 and this is her first official job since they were born. She spoke of the inconvenience of finding she had no form P 45, and of having emergency tax deducted from her long-awaited pay packet.

'While the children were very young I had a variety of casual jobs, and when they were both at school I wound up doing two hours' typing a day and feeling very restless. I wanted a more exciting job for more hours and more money. One day I saw an ad in a paper shop saying: 'kitchen assistant wanted at local school'. The pay was better than I was getting and the hours were from 9.15 until 3.00 pm. This seemed just what I wanted, so I applied and got the job.

Being a kitchen assistant is hard work but I was warned about that, and the work is divided very fairly. We work a rota so that everyone docs a bit of everything — preparing the food, clearing away and washing up. We are so busy that the time goes very quickly.

At my interview, I was told that if all went well I could apply to train as a cook after one month. So I did. As a trainee cook, I had to go to another school. It was an infants' school and it was lovely. The kids were adorable. Christmas was coming and the decorations were up; I saw the nativity play. But for some reason, everything I cooked went wrong! It wasn't for want of trying — I tried everything — but eventually the office said maybe I would be happier in a bigger kitchen. So I went to a boys' school and from then on my cooking was terrific. I had no time to ask what to do. I just had to get on with it. Before, I would stand and wait to be told, which had possibly been the trouble.

Unfortunately, because I had taken on training, I had to be at work at 8.45 am and that meant dropping my kids at a friend's house soon after 8.00. Then the next stage of the training came, when I had to attend a training centre a long way from home. This meant an even earlier start and I decided I couldn't do it. I was sorry to give up. I liked cooking — thought it suited me. The supervisor was very nice about it and said that if I wanted to take it up again I could do so immediately. So here I am, a kitchen assistant again. When the children are older, I might have another try.'

Chapter 6
Shop Work

Introduction

Within the context of the total employment situation, the prospects of finding a job in shop work seem reasonably good. Employment in retail distribution increased from 2,049,300 in 1981 to 2,260,100 in 1985, and there will be a continuing need for staff.

Shop work has many of the characteristics of catering and domestic work. It is fairly widely available locally; there is a high proportion of part-timers, and the industry is very diverse as it is composed of a few 'giants' and a host of smaller firms. It is also work which demands skills which can be learnt on-the-job. Unlike catering and domestic work, however, employment is solely within the private sector.

Throughout retail distribution, more women are employed part-time than full-time, with the greatest concentration (rather than numbers) being found in food and drinks shops where part-timers outnumber full-timers by almost two to one. This is important because, though there may be more general retailing than food shops in your locality, it is in the food shops that you are most likely to find a part-time vacancy. There are significant numbers of men employed part-time, too – and in food and drinks retailing they form a quarter of the total male workforce. This is a proportion that cannot be matched in any other male occupational group working part-time.*

This structure of employment has arisen because most shops stay open for six full days – longer than the full-time working week. Also, retailers have to cope with an uneven demand for their services, so they look to part-timers to help them maintain a balance. Without part-timers, efficient retailing would be virtually impossible. Employees have responded readily to opportunities for part-time work and it might be thought that this coincidence of employers' and employees' needs is most

* These figures are based on the 1981 Census of Employment.

108

fortunate. However, the situation is full of dangers as well as blessings because it appears that part-timers do not gather strength from numbers, but only a clearer identity which enables them to be labelled more easily as a separate group.

There is another danger that attaches to part-time shop work. There is a demand for seasonal staff at such periods as Christmas and the 'sales' which has set a precedent for casual employment. Unscrupulous employers can offer this arrangement to longer-term part-timers who ought more properly to be regular employees. People employed casually are often not 'put on the books' and therefore have no legal status and no possibility of redress against bad treatment. Furthermore, they may themselves infringe the law by failing to pay tax and insurance on the money they earn. This is a situation of which part-timers should beware.

Finding a Job

Large stores seldom advertise for part-time staff as they usually fill their vacancies with people who make a personal inquiry. If you do this, you should ask to see the personnel manager or staffing manager of the branch or store concerned. Small shops advertise jobs at Jobcentres, in the local press, and sometimes in the window of the shop itself. As with many part-time jobs, staff are often found through personal recommendation and word of mouth, so it is worth keeping your ears open and asking friends, particularly those who work in shops, if they know of any suitable vacancies.

Working in Large Stores

Terms of Employment

Part-timers who are engaged as permanent staff will be covered by the provisions of employment law according to the number of hours they work each week (see Chapter 2). Beyond this, they may receive benefits from three sources: Wages Council legislation, negotiated rights and the goodwill of employers.

Wages in retailing are governed by the Retail Wages Councils which set two statutory minimum pay rates for people working in food and non-food retailing. Present minimum amounts (spring 1986) are: food retailing £82.12 (London), £79.62 (elsewhere), and non-food retailing £82.49 (London), £79.99 (elsewhere). These rates apply to people over the age of 19 and are set for a 39-hour week. All employees should receive at least the hourly equivalent of this. The Union of Shop, Distributive and Allied Workers (USDAW) considers these rates the absolute minimum and aims to negotiate a full-time wage of several pounds above these levels. Wages, therefore, may well be higher if you work in a unionised establishment and you will certainly have more chance of equal pay, *pro rata*, with full-timers. Some companies operate a closed shop (whereby all employees must belong to the union), whereas others virtually forbid union activities (although it is illegal, under the Employment Protection Act, to dismiss or discipline workers for trade union activity).

Eligibility for other benefits is usually based on the number of hours you work each week, the general rule being that the more hours you work the more likely you are to qualify for benefits. There is usually a lower hours requirement for paid holidays, maternity leave and sick pay, and a higher one for inclusion in the company pension scheme and any production bonus arrangements. If you work for fewer than eight hours a week, you may lose out on these benefits altogether; above these hours, the thresholds vary from one employer to another, illustrating different degrees of generosity and/or union will and success in negotiating advantageous terms. To take eligibility for pension schemes as an example: Harrods includes all employees working for 20 hours or more a week; Tesco, all those working for 32 hours or more, whereas the John Lewis Partnership, despite its otherwise egalitarian attitude to part-timers, restricts its pension fund to full-time employees only.

As a part-timer, therefore, in some respects you will be a second-class employee, although your value is beyond doubt: you are a money saver. If you work on a Saturday, you could be saving your employer up to £20, which would otherwise be paid as overtime rates to full-time staff. This situation places you in a somewhat anomalous position with the union, USDAW, whose first commitment is to the welfare of its full-time members. USDAW opposes the replacement of full-time staff by part-timers, but the union has a growing number of part-timers in membership and does all it can to look after their rights and pursue the cause of equality for all workers. So it is true to say that, although you may find it more difficult to secure part-time employment in an establishment with a strong union branch, once you are there you will probably get better terms of employment. Incidentally,

USDAW has set up a network of Women's Committees which are currently contributing to, and sponsoring, research into the particular problems facing women members at work. It would be strange indeed if these activities did not throw some light on the more particular problems of part-timers.

Working Conditions
Anyone who has worked in a large shop will know something of the complexity of the organisation, and may have felt the element of showmanship related to shop work which is supported, behind the scenes, by a hierarchical staffing structure. This is especially noticeable in department stores, where each department stages its day's performance under the directorship of the departmental manager. In supermarkets, each section has its supervisor who is responsible for its presentation and subsequent smooth running.

There is, therefore, considerable opportunity in shop work for promotion within the organisation, and this is encouraged by the emphasis placed upon training. Every large retailing company has its own structure of training for supervisory and managerial positions, which makes it possible for anyone with ability to rise from the ranks of the shop floor.

Within this atmosphere, part-timers are something of an anomaly — necessary for the functioning of the organisation but excluded from advancement. As far as can be judged, no retailing company has solved the problem of fitting part-timers into its promotional structure by admitting that a position of any responsibility can be carried out on a shared or part-time basis. The only exceptions to this are the self-contained part-time 'support' jobs such as shelf-filling, where supervisors may be drawn from the ranks of the part-time team.

Part-time jobs, therefore, are the more mundane ones, with no promotion prospects. Even so, in the present unemployment situation, employers can, and often do, demand experience before employing part-timers. In their own interests, however, they will offer training in the skills necessary for the job.

Part-timers are employed either to fill a regular vacancy, or as 'floaters' who fill in where necessary. There is obviously more stability in the former arrangement, and more opportunity to feel satisfaction in doing a job well and forming friendships with colleagues. Floaters are usually employed in the largest stores, and will be consigned to a particular depart-

111

ment so that the stress of constant change is not too great. Some stores offer part-time 'floating' posts to staff who reach retirement age. These posts are usually supernumerary, and all benefits associated with full-time employment cease.

Though the work may be mundane, it can also be interesting! This is especially the case if you like meeting a variety of people and enjoy dealing with customers. It will be very busy, and, as you are likely to be employed at peak times, you may miss the quieter periods which can ease the pressure of work for full-timers.

Under the 1950 Shops Act, no employee can work for more than six hours without a 20-minute break. This is the basic requirement and most full-timers have rest periods in excess of this. The position of part-timers, however, is less certain. Whereas full-time employees have an established pattern of tea and meal breaks, part-timers may be excluded from such arrangements, especially as one of their functions may be to provide cover for these breaks.

The tendency towards increasing employment of part-timers, instigated by employers for economic reasons, has inevitably produced a certain amount of distrust among full-time workers. Part-timers may be viewed critically in some establishments, and their apparent shortcomings made the subject of complaint. Absence is particularly frowned upon, and it may be impossible to explain that the circumstances which make you a part-timer also sometimes cause you to be absent.

One of the great 'perks' of a job in retailing is the opportunity for discount shopping. This is usually available to part-timers, though there will often be an 'hours worked' qualification and you may have to wait until you have been employed for a certain length of time.

Hours of Work
The most readily available are the evening hours (occasionally early morning), during which supermarket shelves are stocked by part-time teams. During opening hours, the greatest need for part-timers is at peak periods — weekends and late shopping nights — and, beyond these, almost any combination is possible. Branches of the major chain stores usually arrange their part-time shifts according to each store's needs, so it is not possible to identify large-scale patterns. Most shifts are pre-arranged

and not liable to alteration, though you may be asked to help out with additional hours at particularly busy periods.

Work Tasks
The tasks you will be asked to perform vary with the style of selling. The demands made on you will be most exacting if you work in a prestige store where customers expect high standards of service. Selling techniques and the technology used to assist them have changed during the last few years, and if you are new to shop work, or have been out of it for some years, there will be new processes you will have to learn. In most of the larger stores, computerised checkouts and cash tills which also record stock levels are used. This has revolutionised stock-taking and reordering routines and, though designed to simplify and streamline these procedures, involves staff in the use of highly technical equipment. You may be required to pick up new skills quickly and with the minimum of instruction, as it is common for part-time staff, employed at the busiest times, to be rushed through training sessions — simply because there is not enough time allowed.

In large stores, the main tasks are taken on by counter-hands, checkout operators, cash till operators, and general shop floor workers who keep an eye on the goods and the customers in a particular section. There are other tasks, slightly more removed from the business of selling but equally essential to the functioning of a store, performed by: porters, security officers and handypersons who are often employed part-time, and usually the rates of pay for these jobs are rather higher.

Working in Small Shops

Terms of Employment
No generalisations can be made about the terms of employment in small shops. They probably range from the best to the worst and will not necessarily bear any relation to the 'class' of the establishment. The corner shop, which badly needs a coat of paint, may provide better terms than the smart boutique. If you work in a small shop, you will be heavily dependent on the goodwill of your employer because you are less likely to have protection and support from other sources. For a start, legislation reduces your protection by exempting employers of fewer than six people from their obligations to reinstate women after maternity leave (see Chapter 2, p 37). Apart from this, you

113

are likely to find union membership more difficult and less rewarding because the union has less power to negotiate on behalf of people working in isolation. Wages Council minimum rates of pay, however, apply to *all* shop workers, wherever they work.

As a permanent employee you are easily exploited, but if you take on work on a casual basis you are even more at risk. Offers of casual employment may be tempting because of the opportunity to work flexible hours, but by employing you in this way your employer frees himself of all obligations to you under employment law and, very possibly, ties you up in an arrangement which is illegal and about which you therefore have no power to complain. You will get no job-security, no sick pay or paid holidays and, often, a very low hourly wage. You may save a little through not paying tax, but you will sacrifice a great deal more in the long run.

These are the pitfalls — the shortcomings of the system — but it would be wrong to suggest that all small employers abuse the freedom they are given. Many are very good to their employees, engaging them on a permanent basis and paying for sick leave and holidays. They are obviously not in a position to provide the range of facilities to be found in a large company. You will not, for instance, have access to an occupational pension scheme — but the consideration a sympathetic boss may give to your personal needs and difficulties can more than make up for this. You cannot expect your terms of employment to be clearly defined on paper (as they would be in a large establishment), but it is best to be certain from the outset about arrangements for hours of work, rates of pay, sick pay, holidays and notice to terminate employment. Above all, you should make sure that you are 'on the books' and, therefore, legally in employment.

Working Conditions
Working in a small shop is quite unlike working in a large store. In most cases it involves traditional selling across the counter, and the minimum of technology. There is much more personal contact with customers who, if the shop is a local one, may be 'regulars' and like to chat to you. In small shops there are few opportunities for separating tasks, and you may find yourself involved to an extent with the whole running of the place. If the relationship between you and your boss is good, the

atmosphere may be one of give and take, with both of you making concessions for the convenience of the other.

If the atmosphere is good, it may seem out of place to insist upon your legal rights. You should, however, have adequate breaks. You are covered by the provisions of the Shops Act 1950 which states that you may not work for six hours without a 20-minute break, and by the Health and Safety at Work Act 1974. You can obtain from your local council information about provisions in this Act which might affect your employment.

CASE STUDIES

Margaret. Shop-floor Supermarket Worker
Margaret has years of experience in part-time shop work of various kinds. She has held her present post for nine years.

'Twelve years ago, when the children were young, I did an evening job filling shelves for Sainsbury's. It was the only time I could work, as my husband was home then to mind the children. I was trained as a supervisor to organise the team. The shift was about three-and-a-half hours if I remember rightly, from 6.00 until 9.30 pm, six days a week. The good thing about it was the pay. You get a higher rate if you work after the store has closed.

My present job is more varied and the daytime hours are more pleasant. I work from 9.00 am until 1.00 pm each day, and I feel that I am lucky to get these hours for the job I am doing. Some stores only employ people on the shop floor for full days — say, two or three a week — and I would not find that so convenient.

I look after a section in Homewear, and this means doing a bit of everything. My main job is to do computer counts for re-ordering stock. The store I work in does not have electronic tills, so this involves counting stock, looking up product numbers and transferring the information on to forms. I do this on Mondays. The information is processed and the new stock arrives about a fortnight later, so you have to plan ahead. I'm also responsible for displaying stock. Again, we are old-fashioned and still lay it out on counters, rather than hanging it. And, of course, I have to set out the new stock when it arrives. In between times, I fill in on the tills during coffee and lunch breaks. All staff are now trained to use the tills so that they can do this. And always, I'm available to help customers and keep an eye on them as well! This is not always as easy as it sounds. The other day there were two small children running round and knocking stock over. When I told them to stop, their parents appeared and were very nasty about it — started threatening to call the manager and get me the sack. Fortunately, another lady customer spoke up for me and left her name and address — so the trouble blew over.

The staff in my store is relatively small, not like superstores where the numbers can run into hundreds. There is one other part-timer on the shop floor and several more working the tills. Our rights and conditions are laid down clearly and, on the whole, they are good. If you work 16 hours or more, after one year you get a 10 per cent discount on goods, and everything *pro rata* with full-timers except inclusion in the pension scheme. I do rather resent that. The company operates a closed shop, which means that we all belong to USDAW. Our union dues are deducted from our wages each week, but we don't have to pay the political precept if we object. We can nominate a charity instead.

I don't object to belonging to a union, but I also think that unions cannot do much for part-timers. If our rights are limited, there seems to be little they can do about it. On the other hand, they can intercede in cases of personal dispute, or unofficial unfairness. I have known cases where they were very helpful in this way — and of others where people in non-unionised shops lost out because they were told to take it or leave it.

I think you need more brains for shop work today than when I started. Like everything, it has become increasingly technical and you have to be able to manage the machines.'

Maureen. Shop Worker

Maureen is a widow who works in a small, family-run local shop.

'I was left with five children to bring up on my own, so any extra money I could earn was always welcome. Years ago, when the children were small, I did homeworking. It was for a charity organisation. I had to fill envelopes with stickers, a leaflet and a dozen cards, and I was paid six shillings a thousand, if I remember rightly. That way, I earned about six pounds a week. It was terrific, that six pounds, but the work just faded out.

I used to go into the shop every day to buy my cigarettes and one day they asked me if I could do some cleaning for them, Fridays. They said I could bring my youngest daughter, who was then a year old, with me. I thought it would be a little bit of extra money so I took it on. That was 14 years ago.

A bit later, they enlarged the shop and I began coming for an hour each day. Finally, they went on holiday and I was asked to help in the shop itself. It became a permanent arrangement and I've served behind the counter from 3.30 until 5.00 pm every day until a few years ago.

Then, my first employers retired and sold the shop, and the new people wanted more help. Now my work hours are 6.30 am until 12.30 pm and 3.30 until 5.00 pm. It's hardly part-time but it suits me now my children are grown-up.

I found it quite easy to adapt to shop work once I knew what the prices were and I got used to the customers. We get the same people in every day and you listen to their aches and pains and troubles. You get all the local gossip as well. People seem to think we know about everything in the area. They ask us where they can buy the things we haven't got, and lorry drivers come in to inquire the way. Also, there's more interest in the work itself. My boss asks my opinion about what to order and so on, and I wouldn't get that in a large place.

116

I suppose you can't better yourself like you could if you were working for a large firm, and if they didn't want to employ me any more I couldn't expect anything like redundancy money.* But I wouldn't like working in a big shop. I don't mix well, really. I'm very quiet and the personal atmosphere suits me fine. Also, my employers are very easy-going. If I want to nip off and we are not busy, they will say, 'Go on, Maureen. Off you go'. And when my hospital appointments come up —I've had quite a bit of illness — they give me time off when a large firm might take it out of my wages. My daughters help in the shop. My boss wouldn't take on anybody, but he'll have them because he knows me. It all works to my advantage and suits me fine.'

Eileen. Manageress of a Second-hand Clothes Shop

Eileen has had a chequered career, beginning as a trainee buyer at Liberty's and running through a series of jobs, mainly in shops, as she struggled to support her children in and out of three failed marriages. Now, at last, she believes she has fallen on her feet.

'As far as working life goes, I've always been insecure. My very first job was a good one with excellent prospects, but it was cut short when I became pregnant. I *had* to get married, as one did in those days (I'm talking about 19 years ago), and after that I went from one job to another.

I was always a mother first. That was all I wanted to be, but circumstances forced me to work. At first, I worked in department stores — the smart ones — but only for a few months at a stretch. Every time a baby-minder let me down, or my child was ill, I gave up my job. That was the only way I could cope. Finally, I had a nervous breakdown and my marriage broke up. My husband took our child and I was alone. I worked for a while as a cinema usherette and it was fine. I was in the dark and I didn't have to see, talk to, or *be* anybody.

Then followed two more relationships, three more children, and a whole host of jobs. I ended up alone once more, but this time I had the children. I worked in a family-run delicatessen — very snob — and I don't think I've been in another place where they treated people so badly. They had a very good number in employing people who were so desperate that they were willing to work on any terms. I worked there for four days a week from 10.00 am until 3.00 pm and they wouldn't put me on the books or give me more hours, though I wanted both. There was only one official and full-time employee; the rest of us were part-timers who came and went at odd hours. I was there from 1979 until early 1982 and I began at £1.10 an hour and was earning £1.30 an hour when I left. I had no pay for sickness or even bank holidays, and on one occasion they decided they didn't want me any more but they didn't even bother to tell me until I turned up for work.

* Maureen was unaware of her right to redundancy pay, and probably would not claim it anyway, as her employers were good to her. The personal relationship was central to her employment situation and when, following this interview, the shop again changed hands, and the new owners proved less sympathetic employers, Maureen gave up her job.

There was nothing I could do about it. Later, I went back — awful as it was, it was convenient to know that because they were employing you in such a casual fashion, you could work in a casual manner. I needed this for emergencies with the children and — the best thing about the job — they were willing to employ students during the school holidays so that I could have time off to spend with my children.

Now, with my present job, I seem to have fallen on my feet. I have joined with a friend and we buy up second-hand furniture and clothing and re-sell it. All the trendy stuff, you know. I manage the shop and the other girl does the buying and makes the contacts. I go in at 10.30 am and open up the place and I'm there until 3.00 pm. I deal with the display, pricing and stock books, and we get together at the weekends to do the accounts and go around the market stalls. I've never been particularly into clothes, but now I'm much more conscious of fashion and what will 'go'.

It's marvellous to have nobody breathing down my neck, and to be able to work flexibly. But on the other hand, everything is up to me and I just cannot take much time off. Recently, for instance, I took my daughter in to work when she was ill and I felt very guilty. She should have been home in bed. But that's the stumbling block for every working mother — what to do when your child is ill. And I still can't accept that every school holiday they have to go to play centre instead of spending their time with me. But as a job it's lovely, and I'm determined to make a go of it.'

Chapter 7

Working in Manufacturing Industries and Agriculture

MANUFACTURING INDUSTRIES

Introduction

The availability of jobs in the manufacturing industries will depend very much on where you live. Overall, less than 10 per cent of workers in manufacturing are part-timers and they work in only a few of the lighter industries. Opportunities are therefore dependent on the location of suitable industries close to where you live, and for this reason they tend to be either easily available, often to the extent of being forged into the community as a way of life, or almost non-existent. Industries most commonly employing part-timers are: food, drink and tobacco, clothing footwear and textiles and toy making. Jobs are also available in light electrical manufacture, in the manufacture of a variety of products involving light assembly work, and in printing.

The manufacturing industries have borne the brunt of the recession and it is here that most jobs have been lost. Proportionately more women than men have been made redundant and redundancies have hit part-timers most of all. It is therefore a contracting job-market and prospects are not good unless you live close to a sizeable factory which relies heavily upon part-time labour. Even if you do, you might find that some part-time shifts are cut. Some factories, for instance, are running shifts for four days instead of five. So if you do find work, it might be for fewer hours than you might have expected.

The manufacturing industries employ part-timers in two ways, as in-workers and as homeworkers, and the two forms of employment will be considered separately. Most of the tasks to be performed under either arrangement require manual dexterity and a certain nimbleness rather than skill; if you have no previous experience, you should find that you can learn the work. Most tasks are repetitive, yet they require a fair degree of

119

concentration. In this sense, part-timers are at an advantage because they are able to sustain the rhythm of work for comparatively short periods.

Finding a Job

Many jobs for both in-workers and homeworkers are found on a 'bush telegraph', whereby an employer may mention that more workers are needed, or an employee that he or she has a friend seeking work. Some factories list vacancies outside their gates, some jobs are advertised in Jobcentres and some even reach the small ads in the local press. But by far the most reliable and thorough method of finding a job is by personal inquiry, both among friends and at the likely firms in your neighbourhood.

Working in a Factory

In factories, part-timers are employed as factory operatives engaged in assembly work and packaging. This may mean sitting at a bench carrying out manual assembly procedures, operating a machine, or working on a continuous process line. Often, your speed of work will be dictated by the speed of the machinery and you must be able to sustain this. On the factory floor, there are only a few supervisors and consequently there will not usually be opportunities for supervisory work.

Terms of Employment

Most employers regard their part-timers as permanent staff, though in the current recession some may offer fixed-term contracts only. In some sections of the food industry — for example, frozen food and canning factories, where the work must be done when the crop is harvested — there is a demand for seasonal labour. The nature of the employment should be made clear to you before you embark on it. In other industries such as printing, where demand is unpredictable, you may find that you can become one of a 'pool' of part-time workers who can be called upon when needed. Work of this kind is on a casual basis and will provide you with no benefits except a wage for the hours you do, but it can be convenient for some people if it occurs with sufficient regularity.

Wages are usually paid at a fixed hourly rate, though sometimes you may be paid piecework rates, particularly in the rag trade or in industries such as printing which call upon workers at busy times. This puts extra pressure on you as your earnings may be very poor if you cannot work speedily. However you are paid, you cannot expect high earnings as the light manufacturing industries are not large money-makers and the jobs done part-time are usually among the lowest paid. Earnings of around £1.80 - £2.50 an hour are the norm.

Many of the industries employing part-timers are covered by Wages Councils (see page 42) and in these there is a set minimum pay rate to which *all* workers are entitled. If you think your wages are suspiciously low, you should check with the Wages Council concerned, and if you are below the minimum pay level you can appeal.

You might find work in a small factory or workshop employing only a handful of people and, if you do, the disadvantages of working for a small employer described in Chapter 6 will apply. (See p 114.) This is the exception rather than the rule, however, as most factories are large enough to support a structure of benefits for the employee and to have well-defined terms of employment.

If you are a permanent employee and work for 16 hours or more a week, you are covered by the provisions of employment law (see Chapter 2, p 33). In addition you will probably get the same hourly rate of pay as full-timers doing the same job. You are also likely to get paid holidays and sick pay in relation to the hours you work and the length of your employment. You may be in an establishment which operates a company pension scheme but your chances, as a part-timer, of being included in it are poor. In factories there are not usually any 'perks' associated with employment. If you work nights the pay may be higher, but there are few opportunities for night work in the industries commonly employing part-timers. Otherwise, the hours you work will be considered as part of your normal part-time shift and you will not receive overtime pay.

Working Conditions

Working in a factory can be dirty, smelly and noisy, but employers often do all they can to minimise the effects of this. Although you will probably be employed to work on a particular section, you can expect to be moved between different processes to give you some variety. Legally, no woman employee can work for more than four-and-a-half hours without

121

a 10-minute break, or more than five hours without a 30-minute break, so this assures women of leisure periods.

One advantage of many jobs in manufacturing is that the pace of work is set by the machines and is therefore the same for every worker. In this situation, part-timers cannot be employed to cope with the busiest times, or expected to work at extra pressure as is so often the case in other occupations. This has an effect on training, too. Most employers are willing to train you in the skills needed for the job, and this training is likely to be less hurried and more adequate because nobody is busier when *you* are working than they are at any other time. People working on a piecework basis, however, will usually find that they can set their own pace of work, and they will tend to pressurise themselves in order to earn more money.

Probably the worst aspect of working in a factory is its potential tedium, but, by all accounts, part-timers cope with this more successfully than full-timers. Perhaps because they remain in the factory for fewer hours, they seem to bring more humour and sociability to their work. It is most common to work in the company of other part-timers, all in a similar position and who appreciate the interlude away from home. So if you value the company as well as the wage-packet, you may find factory work satisfying.

Hours of Work
Work is arranged in shifts, each lasting for four to five hours. Factories employing mainly part-timers have morning (8.00 am to 12.00 noon), afternoon (12.00 noon to 5.00 pm) and sometimes evening (6.00 to 10.00 pm) shifts. These hours are approximate and will vary somewhat from one employer to another. Factories employing mainly full-timers during the day may run part-time evenings shifts to make maximum use of their plant and equipment. As it is more economic for machinery to be kept in continuous operation, work is usually confined to the set shifts and it is rare to be able to work the shortened middle-of-the-day hours (10.00 am to 3.00 pm) which are so convenient for women with school-age children. You must therefore resign yourself either to leaving home early in the morning or to returning home late in the afternoon unless you work an evening shift. However, evening shifts, once a common feature in the light manufacturing industries, are currently being cut back because of the recession.

Part-time Shifts During the Recession
As reports of factory closure and mass redundancy are becoming an everyday feature in the news, the author of this book undertook an inquiry to see how part-time shifts now operating compare with the information available from published sources. Eight companies were contacted and six replied with useful information. They were chosen because they were engaged in forms of production in which a high proportion of part-timers have, in the past, been employed. They consisted of two tobacco companies, three food manufacturers, one light electrical assembly firm and two toy manufacturers. The contact with the tobacco manufacturers was unsuccessful.

Food manufacturing — One firm, manufacturing cereal products, said that it was phasing out part-time employment in response to the economic recession. It considered that 'economically, it makes more sense to employ full-timers . . . as there is the same expense in employing part-timers for less return in terms of work'. As the impression was that the 'expense' referred to was administrative, this seems so negligible that it is doubtful if many employers will be guided by such considerations if it is otherwise in their interests to employ part-timers. Nevertheless, it is an attitude which cannot be discounted, and may be wide-spread enough to contribute to the reduction in part-timers in the manufacturing industries.

The other two companies, by contrast (one confectionery, and one biscuit manufacturer), employed mainly part-timers and intended to continue doing so. One, however, restricted this intention to women, as it had discontinued employing male part-timers who had been mainly pensioners, in order to create more full-time jobs for younger men. Both stressed that part-time working was the established pattern in their factories and, therefore, was generally accepted. Part-timers were offered benefits *pro rata* and, in the confectionery firm, were even included in the pension scheme. There was a variety of working shifts — in the biscuit company a few people worked shortened, mid-day hours — and both firms ran an evening shift. In the confectionery firm, part-timers could become supervisors on the evening shift.

Electrical manufacturing — The electrical company stressed that it was reducing its workforce during the current recession. It has cut out part-time shifts during the day and is now only operating an evening part-time shift from 5.30 pm to 9.00 pm.

Workers on this shift are offered a three-month contract in the expectation that the arrangement will last for at least a year. Full-time supervisors oversee alternate shifts to ensure continuity with the daytime work.

Toy manufacturing — One firm had cut out part-time work during the day but was continuing an evening shift from 6.00 to 10.00 pm to make the fullest use of production machinery. Evening workers were permanent employees doing 20 hours a week with entitlement to paid holidays *pro rata.*

The other firm was also feeling the effects of the recession but had responded differently. It had cut out the evening shift and retained morning and afternoon part-time shifts to continue its practice of employing mainly part-timers. The company operated a sick-pay scheme for part-time workers and gave other benefits *pro rata*, but it had been forced to cut down on other concessions. In the past, women had been allowed to take off the school summer holidays, and students had been employed in their place. This no longer happened, and all workers were restricted to a fortnight's holiday during the annual summer shut-down, with an additional week to be taken at a time convenient to the company.

So, it would seem that part-timers can expect to feel the effects of the recession in a general reduction of job opportunities, of choice in working shifts, and of some concessions which they may previously have been offered. However, this gloomy view of part-timers in manufacturing is not the entire picture. Factories which have employed part-time workers in some numbers seem to regard them sympathetically and to value their services, although the status of their jobs is low. Several employers spoke of the high productivity of their part-time shifts which they attributed to the higher motivation of part-timers, whom they generally considered to be more intelligent than people on full-time shifts. All sorts of people, apparently, work part-time in the manufacturing industries. Out-of-work solicitors, ex-managers, secretaries and a geography teacher were mentioned among the workers who made up the 'interesting variety of people' on part-time shifts.

Homeworking

Homeworking is mainly, though not entirely, a feature of the manufacturing industries. The terms of employment relating to homeworking appear in Chapter 3 so, to avoid unnecessary repetition, this section will be restricted to consideration of the practical obstacles to becoming a homeworker, and the everyday effects on the individual of doing this type of work. The reader should, however, be reminded that this is an extremely insecure and often ill-paid form of employment.

Most homeworking is carried out for the clothing industry, but many other industries also employ homeworkers. They are most needed by those industries which experience a fluctuating seasonal demand for their products — toy making and Christmas 'novelties' are good examples. So availability of work may depend both on the location of a suitable manufacturer and on the time of year at which you make your inquiries.

Methods of Work
You do not usually need any experience to become a homeworker. The test will be in the results of your work. The most usual practice is for your employer to bring you a consignment of work and an example of the finished product. You must copy this, by whatever method you think best. You will probably arrive at your method by trial and error, first achieving a satisfactory result — necessary if you hope to be given more work! — and then finding ways of increasing your speed. Homeworkers are paid piecework rates, so time means money. Although you will be using your own space, electricity and heat, you will probably get a lower rate of pay than you would as an in-worker.

Working Conditions
Working conditions are, in several respects, the exact opposite of those for factory workers. Although you will have the benefit of choosing your own hours of work, you will be denied a change of scene and the social contact with fellow workers. You will probably be remote from the source of your work. As work is delivered to you and then collected, you may never visit the factory which employs you and it is even possible to work without knowing with certainty who your employer is. Your pace of work will not be dictated by conditions outside, so the temptation is for you to work at pressure all the time to increase your earnings. And if plenty of work is available, you may find it difficult to stop working. What you took on as a part-time job may grow until it fills all your available time and takes over your life.

It is easy to see your rewards only in terms of the weekly pay packet and not in terms of the number of hours you have worked to earn it. A few hours here and there each day for six or seven days a week quickly mount up, and if related to the wage you receive may reveal a surprisingly low hourly rate.

Unlike other forms of work, homeworking impinges directly on your domestic life. You may have machinery to accommodate; you will certainly have equipment and the work itself. If you have young children, you will have the problem of preventing them from interfering with your work. In fact, there are very real health and safety hazards to be considered. At home, you are outside the scope of the Health and Safety at Work Act 1974, so no checks are made upon whether the noise, dust, fluff, the smell of glue, etc might be injurious to you or your family. You will have to decide on these matters for yourself, and weigh them against the advantages, or sheer necessity, of earning money which you might otherwise be unable to earn.

CASE STUDIES

Molly, Factory Operative
Molly has three teenage children, and works in a brush factory.

'With children, you can't work full-time. I've had all sorts of jobs and this is the worst, in the brush factory. But it's just round the corner and the hours, from 9.00 am until 4.30 pm, are convenient, so I stay. I've been in the job for seven years and I wouldn't mind a change, but you get into a rut and it's difficult to put yourself somewhere different. I've heard of a job machining from 10.00 till 3.00 and I'd be interested in that. I might go and see them.

I've done cleaning and before this, I had a short time machining in a handbag factory. That was quite pleasant and the people were nice, but the money was not that good. Then I had an operation and, for a while, it was too much to work at all, so I gave it up.

In my present job, it's stuffy and noisy and dirty with the machines always going. I work on a machine which mixes and sorts the bristles. Then I have to bundle them. It's a hard job. I have to get them all even and it's terrible!

My husband works, but we still need the money I earn. Also, I like to work. I come from the West Indies and I wouldn't like to think I was getting unemployment money in this country.'

Sue, Machinist
Sue has two children aged six and eight. Two years ago she gave up homeworking as a machinist. Her story illustrates how

working unconventional hours can make long hours of work seem like a part-time job.

'I've tried all sorts of things. I've been a representative for sales promotion parties and, if I look back on my life, that is one of the things I will remember. The parties were to promote ladies' 'novelties' and I went to the first one just for a laugh, with friends. There wasn't anything rude about it. Some of the things on sale were rude, but we just laughed, and it wasn't obscene, or anything. We all drank coffee and it was a really good ladies' night. The representative at that party said I should try it because the reps get a percentage of the party takings. So I phoned up and got my kit together. I must stress that I wouldn't go to strangers. I took the gear to my friends, starting with the ones I knew best and, in that way, I made quite a lot of money. I did it for three months just before Christmas. It's not the sort of thing you could do for too long.

My longest experience of homeworking was as a machinist. I did it for about a year. I was not an experienced machinist, but my sister was doing machining and she gave me a number to phone. I never knew the name of the company. Everything was delivered to me and I got cash in hand at the end of the week. I was given one of the firm's machines which went like the wind. An ordinary home machine would not be fast enough, or stand up to the wear and tear.

At first, I was given simple dresses to make at 50p a time and then I was put on to more complicated work. Every time I was given a new design I'd have a sample to copy, but I had to work out how best to do it. There were no instructions. I adapt to new things easily so I found that I was earning good money quite quickly.

The trouble with homeworking is that it really gets a hold on you. I would take the kids to school and rush home to finish my housework so that I could start machining. When you know that more time means money, you can't stop. My husband hated it because I didn't want to go out and I'd be sitting machining at midnight. Of course, the big advantage is that you can organise your own hours which is essential when you have very young children — and fine if you know when to stop!

You can earn a lot machining. Some people can earn £80 a week in their hand.* My worst week was £30, and a good week a bit over £50 (1981). For that, I used to work from 6.00 pm until midnight every evening, and a couple of hours in the afternoon as well. My boss was very good to me. He always gave me work immediately I asked for it, and if I told him I was going on holiday he'd slip me £10 and tell me to keep quiet about it. Then, one day, he said that we must start paying tax — he was starting with all his homeworkers — and I thought for that kind of money I could do sensible hours. Also, my youngest had started school by this time and I was free to work during the day. So I gave up and found a part-time office job. I'm still in that job.'

* This was in 1983.

AGRICULTURE

Agriculture is a production industry, not a manufacturing industry; nevertheless it fits most easily into this chapter. It is the largest single industry in the UK, currently employing 356,600 workers of whom 32,500 women work part-time (*Employment Gazette*, March/April 1986). There has been a slight drop in the total number of employees since the Census of Employment of 1981.

Despite the relatively high proportion of part-timers, it is doubtful if the opportunities for permanent part-time workers are correspondingly plentiful because the greatest need in agriculture is for seasonal workers. The best chance of finding a stable staffing situation is in glasshouses, where the seasons are bypassed and there is a steady flow of work. Otherwise, small farmers and horticulturalists may have a need for regular part-time help. Wages for agricultural workers are set by the Agricultural Wages Board (currently around £90 for a 40-hour working week) and you should get the correct rate *pro rata.*

Seasonal work is usually paid at piecework rates and will vary in its frequency according to what is cultivated in your locality. Fruit farming probably offers the greatest frequency, followed by mixed vegetable cultivation, with cereal crops coming last. A combination of fruits provides a prolonged harvesting season, lasting from June until the autumn. This is when part-time work is available. There are also opportunities for work during the spring pruning season. Harvesting is always the time of greatest activity, whatever the crop, and though some processes are now carried out by machines there is still a good deal of hand picking. The activity is pleasant, if monotonous, and it is possible to take children with you.

It is difficult to earn a steady income through seasonal work because of the lull during the winter months. To support yourself in this way, you need to be a Jack-of-all-trades, and turn your hand to something different when there is no work on the land. All work of this type is casual, so you will have no benefits of employment apart from the pay for the work you do. Because of the prevalence of casual work in the industry, some employers extend this arrangement to more regular forms of employment. If you seek permanent employment, and manage to find it, you should check that it is just that. You should be 'on the books' as an official employee and then, if you work for 16 hours or more each week, you have protection under employment law.

Finding a Job

Employers often advertise in the local press for help during the busiest seasons. Jobs of a more regular kind may be advertised in Jobcentres. Once again, however, the most reliable way of finding steady work is through word of mouth, and it will be particularly helpful in the most rural areas if you have connections with agriculture or horticulture and are known locally. People like to employ people they know.

Chapter 8

Office Work

Introduction

Office workers do not appear as a separate occupational group in employment statistics, so there is no easy way of assessing whether part-time opportunities are on the increase or the decline. Office workers as a whole must be feeling the effects of the recession (local councils, for instance, are trying to save on administrative costs) but it is unclear whether employers are responding to the situation by dispensing with part-timers, or realising that they may, in many cases, be the more cost-effective option. In any event, it seems unlikely that there will be a dramatic reduction in the number of part-time jobs because, in an occupation where women predominate, there will always be a high rate of full-time labour loss.

In general, it seems that firms of any size, whose offices merely support the main occupation rather than form an integral part of it, manage to find enough full-timers for their needs. Retailing and manufacturing companies rarely employ part-timers in their offices. Small firms, however, often have need of a part-time contribution to their more modest administrative load. Apart from these, the main opportunities exist in organisations which have administration as their primary function, because staff are needed in such numbers that there would be a shortage of labour if part-timers were not employed. Examples of such organisations are banking and insurance firms, local government and, to a certain extent, the Civil Service. There is a steady need, too, for part-timers in the health services – hospital secretaries, doctors' receptionists and so on.

Office work spans a wide range of skills, from clerks and receptionists to bookkeepers, personal secretaries, and people who specialise in other administrative procedures. In view of the fact that most tasks can be adapted easily to part-time working, and that there is a distinct advantage for many firms in employing the more specialised workers part-time, employers have proved strangely reluctant to accept part-timing as a common arrangement. This may be because they dislike to see desk spaces and equipment standing empty, and are more inclined to relate their staffing needs to factors of accommodation than to consideration of the work which needs to be done. Whatever the reason, most part-time opportunities occur at the lower levels of work (for clerks, receptionists and copy typists), and are found in greatest numbers within job-splitting arrangements (see Chapter 3, p 56) which solve the problem of wasted accommodation by the expedient of having two workers sharing the same desk, working alternate weeks. There is no quarrel with the principle of this, but more flexibility in hours of work would be appreciated by many people.

Office work has undergone great changes over the past few years because of the new technology. Modern equipment has changed many of the tasks, and the skills needed to perform them. The audio typist has taken over from the shorthand typist and the wordprocessor has revolutionised typing. Telex has arrived as a common piece of office equipment, switchboards are more complex and many procedures are now computerised. In large offices, methods of keeping records have completely changed the previous role of the filing clerk.

Although this may seem frightening if you have been out of office work for some time, it has, in the main, the effect of de-skilling many of the tasks. Once you have learnt to use a machine, you will find that you do not need the expertise that was previously required of you. Technology has its effect on working relationships too, as communication can be by remote control and there is less need for personal contact. The day may soon come when many office workers will have no need to communicate, except with their machines, and you can be sure that such routine jobs will be the ones offered to part-timers. In the meanwhile, however, typing is still the backbone work of the office, and this is the main skill you will need for a part-time job.

Finding a Job

You can find out about jobs in the following ways: through employment agencies (look them up in the Yellow Pages), at Jobcentres (see p 181), in the local press, and through friends or past employers. Temping can sometimes lead to a permanent appointment and you can make a direct inquiry to organisations employing a large proportion of part-timers — banks, insurance companies, local councils etc. Part Time Careers Ltd (see p 188) tests all applicants in office skills and ensures that they go to permanent appointments with the same pay and fringe benefits, *pro rata*, as full-timers.

Re-training

If you have not been at work for some years, and feel that your office skills have grown rusty, you should be eligible for free training, sponsored by the Manpower Services Commission, to brush up your skills and familiarise yourself with new technology. Your local Jobcentre will tell you how to apply. For further details, see page 181.

Working Conditions

Many part-time office workers feel that they are 'put upon' by being expected to work at greater pressure than full-timers or to stay beyond their hours to get work finished. This is probably because, unless they are working a job-split, or providing cover as a receptionist, their working hours are not arranged in shifts or sessions but are arrived at somewhat arbitrarily. In this situation, it is easy for employers to have a hazy (and optimistic) idea of the amount of work that can reasonably be done in the time allowed.

Further proof of the extra pressure upon upon part-timers in offices is found in the fact that they are among the most disadvantaged in terms of meal and tea breaks. There are no statutory regulations governing provision of breaks, except for shop and factory workers, but all full-timers are allowed rest and meal periods, whereas part-timers are often required to work without a break. If you are on your feet a lot, this can be very tiring and if you work a long morning, finishing at 2.00 pm, sheer hunger can make the last hour extremely unpleasant. When you apply for a job, you should not assume that you will get a break, if the conventional time for lunch, tea etc falls within your hours.

Although most part-timers are employed in clerical and lower secretarial grades, there are precedents for aspiring to appointments in higher positions. Part Time Careers Ltd of London, the only employment agency in the UK dealing solely with part-time appointments, has had success in finding people high-grade posts, though most of them are in central London. The agency believes that part-time employment can provide the answer for many employers who need specialist services but on a small scale, and the response received suggests that more part-time work of this nature could be operated in other parts of the country.

The question of status is always an important one for the part-timer because, as long as part-timers are confined to the low grades and routine jobs, their image with colleagues will suffer. In very small offices it is possible to overcome this by becoming the proverbial 'treasure', the Jack-of-all-trades who will always save the day in an emergency. But in large offices it is hard not to feel that you are on the sideline. Office jobs are not usually self-contained and it can be difficult to measure your achievement if you receive no acknowledgement of it. This makes job satisfaction low for many people.

Terms of Employment
Casual work is less common in offices than it is in other settings, so most people will be regarded as permanent staff. However, some people working alternate week job-splits have their contracts terminated at the end of each week they work and resumed at the beginning of the next. As this deprives them of continuity of employment, which is a prerequisite for benefiting from the provisions of employment law as well as for various State social benefits, it is something which anyone taking on this form of employment should take into account.

Large companies operating job-splitting schemes generally grant the staff involved the same pay and holidays *pro rata* as full-timers and identical maternity leave and pay. Entitlement to sick leave may be different, however, and part-timers are not usually included in the companies' pension schemes. Employers in the public sector usually give *pro rata* pay and benefits. However, there has been a long wrangle in local government, one of the largest employers of part-time women workers, about the superannuation scheme. It is about ten years since employers and unions agreed that part-timers should be brought in, but successive governments rejected the proposals on the grounds of cost. At long last, however, they were admitted in April 1986. There are other disadvantages, too. Many councils are anxious to benefit from the government grants for splitting jobs, but to do so they must employ people who are unemployed or would otherwise be made redundant. This, in practice, means that they are proposing to offer split jobs only at the basic clerical grade. NALGO, the union involved, is opposing this in favour of broadly defined job-sharing — that is, part-time opportunities at any level.

NALGO has shown a concern for its women members and, among them, the part-timers. In 1983 it engaged upon research and the findings showed that although there are agreements on paper that part-timers in local government should have *pro rata* benefits, employers find ways around this. Instances include low grading irrespective of work undertaken, and lack of time off for training and personal matters such as doctors' visits, children's school visits and so on — there is a feeling that they should do this in their *own* time. These do reveal an attitude of grudgingness rather than generosity towards part-timers. Without comparable research, it is impossible to say if the attitude of most private employers is any different.

The result of informal inquiries, however, leads to the conclusion that many of the smallest employers are very generous to their part-timers. As a group, small employers tend to dislike unions, so it is probably best to rely on the paternalism of your boss — as long as things go well.

Hours of Work

Office work is associated with the hours from nine to five, so it might seem reasonable to assume that part-time office work involves working a proportion of these hours. In some cases, it does. Many women find jobs in which they can work the coveted shorter day from, for example, 9.30 until 3.00. But many work the alternate week system, which means a full day's work during the week when you work, and many more find themselves working unsocial hours. There is plenty of scope for working during evenings — mainly as receptionists in hotels, doctors' and dentists' surgeries and other places that stay open late. It is even possible to work at night. Such hours are unpopular with full-timers, so they become a part-time job. You will not often find that you are paid more to work unsocial hours, so your decision must rest on their convenience as far as your personal circumstances are concerned.

CASE STUDIES

Penny, General Office Worker
Penny has one child aged 7 and works in the office of a small manufacturing firm.

'I've worked at the same place ever since I left school at the age of 16. I left to have a baby and went back two years later to work part-time from 10.00 am until 2.00 pm each day.

It is a family firm and very friendly. People stay for a long time, and everyone gets the proverbial gold watch after 25 years. One man has been working here for 57 years. Our boss is a county councillor and he treats us well. He pays me very generously. I don't think he could pay me double if I worked full-time. I've been back for five years and my wages are more than twice what they were at first.

When I worked full-time I was a plain invoice clerk and I went back part-time as a secretary. Then my old boss died, and now I'm in reception, doing the switchboard, typing and telex. I'm also the filler-in. If anybody's on holiday I help out, and I tend to find myself doing all the bits and pieces no one else wants to do. I prefer it, as it gives me more variety.

I had to learn to use the switchboard and the telex and they were willing to teach me. I also think I would get promotion although I'm part-time. But I realise I'm more fortunate than most. The only dis-advantage is that as I'm a part-timer they think nothing of asking me to stay a bit longer to finish a job. That didn't happen when I worked full-time.

I went back to work from choice. When I was at home I wasn't a type that went out and found life, so I only saw my husband and my mother each day. I wanted to see people and have someone else to talk to, and my mother jumped at the chance of looking after my daughter while I was away. Now, we couldn't do without the money I earn, so sometimes I feel caught and think I'd like to be able to give it up. But it's such a busy job. I'd probably be bored at home.'

Annette, Audio Typist

Annette is a single parent with a child of 7. She works in a medium-sized office in the public sector.

'This is my first part-time job and I began it when my son started school. Up till then he'd been at a day nursery where he could stay until five o'clock and I was able to work full-time. We are both com-pletely dependent on my income.

Originally I was a qualified secretary, and I did a lot of 'temping'. I would really have liked to stay on at school and do an art course but I come from a large family and money was short, so I left after one year in the sixth form. After my son was born, I didn't work for 18 months. Then, when he went to nursery, I got a full-time job working at a college in the administration of their exams. I found that people were not terribly sympathetic about things like children being ill. If I stayed home with my son I had to lie to get my salary at the end of the month. I felt sick having to do it at first, but I learned in the end. I've been reading a book about women in the last century and my impression is that not an awful lot has changed.

Even before I left full-time work, my impression of part-timers was that they worked a bloody lot harder. Also, when you arrive and leave at a different time from the others, you are always seen and you can't fiddle your hours to get off a bit earlier. When you start looking for part-time work, there's not an awful lot of choice, and you have to consider things that are beneath your station — salary-wise as well as other things. You are restricted to jobs with hours that fit and have to be close to home in case there's an emergency with your child. I would even have taken a copy typing job, and I took the audio typing on as a temporary measure until I found something better. But, these days, good jobs are rare and I'm still there three-and-a-half years later.

Really, I'm very frustrated with what I'm doing and peeved about the pay and about feeling that I'm always being taken for granted. I'm particularly interested in history and I'd like to take a course in history, but I couldn't stand the thought of being in financial shit for several years. I feel I've got to give my son as much as others get. He mustn't be different. So, lack of money stops me trying something new and, even now, it dogs me. I get Family Income Supplement and rent and rates rebates, but all the time I'm means-tested. I'm forever declaring my poverty and I hate it.'

Jenny. Clerical and Administrative Worker with the BBC

Jenny trained as a secretary. She has two children aged 6 and 9 and works a part-time job-share with a friend. They both work daily from 9.00 am until 1.00 pm, Jenny taking the school term weeks and her friend working during the holidays.

'I had a variety of part-time jobs when the children were small. It was not always easy to find part-time work, so some of the jobs were fairly boring. Eventually, I started working for the BBC as a 'floater' — that is, a freelance worker who comes when required — on a local radio station.

When a part-time permanent post became vacant, a friend and I decided that we could do it between us as she was happy to work only in the school holidays and I could manage every day during term time. We put our proposition to the BBC and it was accepted — but only on a continuing freelance basis. We were not offered a permanent appointment.

It has worked quite well for three years now. We are paid weekly and the pay quite simply goes to whoever has worked that week. Nobody minds which of us it is as long as the work gets done. We *never* divide a week because that would be too complicated. Of course, we have no job security or other benefits, but beggars can't be choosers!

I find the work interesting. We arrange the content of the afternoon phone-in programmes. Everything is pre-planned. We sift through the people who want to participate, make a selection, and then arrange it with them. Sometimes we get the opportunity to do interviews — there's more pay for that — but I find that part-timers are not encouraged to make an extra contribution. Full-timers tend to see them as taking away their work.

I've never had any of my own money unless I've earned it. So I must work. But I believe you don't get anywhere unless you work full-time, which I cannot do. You have to be more conscientious as a part-timer, because you are less easily accepted. My job with the BBC is very busy and I enjoy that. But to my full-time colleagues I'm just a person who comes, does, and then goes.'

Gloria. Secretary Bookkeeper

Gloria works for Part Time Careers Ltd. She was a single parent and, while she was bringing up her daughter, worked full-time for the sake of the salary. Later, she seized upon the opportunity to work part-time.

The extraordinary thing is that I didn't work part-time before. I thought about it 10 or 12 years ago and made some inquiries, but, at the time, the pay was not enough. Instead, I found myself in a job with some bookkeeping and I took to it like a duck to water. I did some evening study and then I went to work for a firm of American lawyers. It was a very demanding job. I began as secretary bookkeeper and ended up as office manager. The atmosphere was very tense and fraught, so after about four years I decided to throw it in.

My daughter was grown-up so at last I had the freedom to do such a thing. I had no idea what I was going to do. I needed *some* income because I don't have any private means. I went on holiday, and when I returned I became involved in work for my church. There was a new priest with ideas about community involvement and this generated the work. But it soon developed into full-time again, and I didn't want this. I found it became too commercial and I was losing the spiritual side.

So I looked in the Yellow Pages, found Part Time Careers, and here I am! I work four days a week from 10.00 am until 4.00 pm, and the fifth I spend on church work. It is the perfect balance. I wanted to work in the West End of London because I like the shops and I find the atmosphere stimulating. It keeps you alive a bit.

I've been here four months now and the time has flown. In a small agency like this the flow of work is not even. There are quiet times, and others when the phone does not stop ringing. It is very interesting and satisfying work. Also, I have more time for myself than I have done for years, and looking to the future (I'm 50 now) this seems the perfect way of easing into retirement. I take a long time to adjust to change and I couldn't take a sudden ending of my working life.

I'm a more relaxed and happier person since starting part-time work.

Anne. Medical Receptionist

Anne has two children aged 8 and 12. She trained as a secretary and, after the children were born, did a variety of jobs, mostly on a temporary or casual basis. Recently she took a degree in English, but has failed to find a job which would seem to be a natural progression from that.

'I work at a private clinic where people are referred for specialist treatment. We have over 40 doctors registered, all coming and going at different times. The receptionists are the shop front. We spend our time being nice to people — welcoming them, making sure they see the right doctor in the right room, booking their appointments and answering their questions.

137

There are 12 telephones, and sometimes three or four go at once — all for trivial things usually, but it's still very confusing. I answer six million queries a day. I also prepare the rooms and tidy up afterwards. This means sterilising instruments and laying them out again, straightening furniture, putting out clean towels and so forth. It's all very menial. I don't do any clerical work because there are secretaries employed to do that.

I work two mornings a week from 8.45 until 1.00 pm and one afternoon from 1.45 until 6.15. Usually, it's up to half an hour later when I leave because there's an unspoken agreement that no one leaves until the work is finished. Nobody seems to mind because it's meant to be a privilege to work here. The other receptionists are older women, with husbands in comfortable jobs, and they don't need the money. They do it for the privilege and I do it for the money!

The terms of employment are clearly set down. For the first three months you are on probation and are paid £1.75 an hour. For the next two, you get £1.85 an hour, and after that you get all of £2.00! Actually, I think it's very fair — the going rate — because I met a woman who works as an NHS receptionist and she gets £1.85 an hour (1983 figures). We also have quite generous sick pay and three weeks and three days' paid holiday.

Interestingly enough, they employ five of us so that we each work 13 or 14 hours and our pay doesn't come up to the tax threshold, or something. I don't know about job security but there's a friendly atmosphere and I can't imagine them throwing us out for no reason at all.'

Chapter 9
The Health Care Professions

Introduction

A great many disciplines contribute to the provision of health care and it is beyond the scope of this book to deal in detail with them all. However, it is possible to set them within four main groups. Most people are employed within the National Health Service and will find that their terms and conditions of service are clearly laid down. The information given in this chapter relates to NHS work except in a few cases where private sector employment is extensive enough to deserve mention.

Nursing

Two main conditions characterise nursing: it is a female-dominated occupation and, in most cases, it involves 24-hour cover. Both conditions have a significant influence on the opportunities for part-time work.

Part-timers have consistently formed a large proportion of the nursing workforce. Forty per cent of all nurses work part-time. Lately, a few health authorities have initiated job-splitting schemes to provide posts for newly qualified nurses, both in the interests of economy and, no doubt, to benefit from the Government grants now offered for exercises of this kind. It is too early to judge the effect this might have on the position of people who want part-time employment, but many health authorities and hospital groups do not envisage a significant reduction in their need for part-time help in the foreseeable future. However, there may be large regional differences, so your chances of a job will depend to some extent on where you live.

Returning to Work
Because of the difficult hours involved in nursing, it is unusual for nurses to work throughout their childbearing years without a break. Many part-timers, therefore, will be 'returners' needing to re-learn their skills and adapt to the changes which have

139

occurred during their absence. Most of the re-learning involves becoming used to new drug regimes and the use of modern equipment and is not too onerous a prospect. Many returners will welcome the way in which the use of 'disposables' has eased away some of the old tasks.

Until the unemployment situation worsened, many health authorities ran 'Back to Nursing' courses on a regular basis, but few now do so. Some courses are still run, but on an *ad hoc* basis depending on demand, either by the authority or by individual hospitals. They are not usually advertised, so it will be up to *you* to discover *them*. The Senior Nurse (Personnel) of your local health authority should be able to help you. Otherwise, returners may be given some form of orientation training on-the-job, but for bank nurses this may be of a very informal nature.

Re-training

The experience of a time away from work often leads people to want to branch out. If you want to train as a nurse from scratch your prospects are not good. Nursing courses are demanding of both energy and time. There are, however, several part-time courses available; inquiries should be made to the English National Board Careers Advisory Centre.

Training for community nursing specialisations (available only to qualified nurses) takes place at recognised training centres and lasts for set periods as follows: health visiting (registered nurses only), one year; district nursing, six months followed by three months' practical experience; midwifery, two years (three-year courses available to people without nursing qualifications). Courses, however, are full-time and most people expecting to train part-time will have difficulty in meeting the time requirements.

Within the hospital service, many hospitals run courses for nursing specialities such as intensive care, geriatric nursing, operating department nursing, and so forth, under the auspices of the Joint Board of Clinical Nursing Studies. Although possession of a specialist qualification may increase your competitiveness in seeking a post, it is unlikely to have any influence on the variety of hours at which you will be required to work.

Most hospitals and nursing centres will have a list of courses available locally.

Finding a Job

Nursing agencies will offer you the easiest route to work, but agency work rarely turns into permanent employment. Part-time jobs are not often advertised, so your best line of inquiry is direct to the nursing officer of your local hospital or, for a more general picture of local opportunities, to the Senior Nurse (Personnel) of your district health authority.

Hospital Nursing

For hospital nurses, the provision of 24-hour cover presents certain difficulties in arranging working hours. If part-timers are employed to work regular hours, and these fall within the more desirable times, this will quite naturally cause resentment among full-timers who must take their turn at both the popular and the unpopular shifts. In practice, therefore, the opposite tends to be the case, and part-timers are often employed to work the unpopular shifts.

The concentration of part-timers into such shifts is not necessarily evidence of discrimination against them, though this may, to some extent, be the case. It is as much an illustration of their own inability to work the variety of hours otherwise required. Most hospitals employ part-timers on a permanent basis to work a specific number of hours, but, in the interests of fairness, the hours must be woven into the normal pattern of shifts. Although this form of employment will give you more security, more job satisfaction through continuity, and a greater degree of integration into the life of your hospital, it will require you to be away from home on shifts operating around the clock. For this reason, many people fall back on night work as the only possible alternative.

There are arguments both for and against night duty. It will keep you in touch with nursing and provide an income through your chosen occupation. It is also less pressurised than daytime work, though when a rush occurs it is almost always in the form of an emergency. On the other hand, the form of employment offered is usually insecure, and it can have a disastrous effect on your personal life if you work with frequent night shifts. The experience of social workers working in hospital settings is that regular night duty nurses find a great strain imposed on their marital relationships, regardless of their family situation when they began work.

TERMS OF EMPLOYMENT

There are various options open to part-timers, and the degree of flexibility within each will be a matter for the individual hospital to decide. Each hospital organises the deployment of part-timers to suit its own needs, but the following pattern is fairly typical:

Permanent part-time staff — You will be employed on a particular ward for an agreed number of hours (eg 3 x 8 hours weekly), but must take your turn at all shifts on a rota system. You will have access to some form of re-orientation training if necessary, and to the Service Training Department for periodic in-service training sessions. Pay and benefits are *pro rata* with full-timers, but your promotion prospects will be limited as long as you continue to work part-time.

The nursing bank — Your name will be entered on a list kept by a particular hospital and you will be employed within it as a floating helper where and when you are needed. The hospital will accept responsibility for offering you work when it can, and you will undertake the hours you can manage. Most demand is for help during unpopular shifts and, as you may be unable to work during public holidays and other 'family' times, you will probably find yourself working nights.

The disadvantage of this form of employment is that you are not a permanent employee, so you have no job security, or guarantee of a regular income. You will receive no benefits apart from a wage for the hours you actually work. As a bank nurse, you are outside the promotional structure of nursing.

Agency nurses — All hospitals call on established agencies at times of staff shortage, though they dislike doing so because of the unknown quality of the nurses sent to them. This is temping (see Chapter 3) and, though you may enjoy the variety for a while, you will miss out on the sense of 'belonging' that many nurses appreciate. Demand for agency nurses is greatest at holidays times and, of course, for unpopular shifts. Private hospitals and clinics are considerable employers of agency nurses and some may pay high rates.

Community Nursing

The increased emphasis on community care has brought about an expansion of job opportunities in the field. Nurses are employed by general practitioners and in schools and industry;

dentists employ dental surgery assistants; registered nurses can take further training to become health visitors, district nurses and midwives. All these jobs (except for midwifery) have the advantage that work is confined to daytime hours, but they are less numerous than hospital posts and competition for them is probably greater. As nurses in the community work in small units, it is not possible to generalise about the arrangements offered to part-timers, except to say that the situation does not lend itself to use of part-time help during unsocial hours, and prospects for people with specialist training may be enhanced by the fact that many primary health care teams may find a part-time contribution sufficient for their needs.

The Paramedical Professions

Paramedical occupations are too numerous to be examined individually in any detail, so comments will be restricted to general observations and the reader is referred to the Council for Professions Supplementary to Medicine, Park House, 184 Kennington Road, London SE11 4BU, for further information. In addition, the addresses of the professional organisations of the disciplines most commonly employing part-timers are listed at the back of this book.

Like nursing, the paramedical professions are female-dominated and therefore experience a high rate of staff loss. On the whole, methods of work do not change fast enough to place returners at a great disadvantage and it is possible to adapt to changes with a little help.

In the past, part-time working was a significant feature of employment but assertions about the ready availability of part-time work should, perhaps, be viewed with some caution. Economies within the NHS have inevitably resulted in job losses which have had their effect on part-time opportunities.

The most significant occupational areas for part-time work are likely to be chiropody, occupational therapy, orthoptics, physiotherapy, radiography, dispensing and ophthalmic optics and speech therapy. In the past, refresher courses were available with some regularity, but these have mostly gone the way of the 'Back to Nursing' courses mentioned on page 140 and orientation training is likely to be of a more informal nature.

Within the hospital service, most work is sessional and easily adapted to part-time working, even if lacking flexibility in hours. There is not the problem of 24-hour cover and the

143

consequent tendency for part-timers to be trapped in unpopular sessions. Part-timing is well established, and pay and benefits are *pro rata* with full-timers, but promotion prospects are limited.

Where specialisation is possible, this may increase your competitiveness, and therefore your choice. Inquiries should be made to the appropriate professional body.

Private practice is a significant part of employment in some occupations — notably chiropody and dispensing and ophthalmic optics — and as long as profits maintain their present level, economies and attendant job losses will not be so much of a feature as they are currently within the NHS.

Finding a Job

For jobs with the NHS your local health authority is the best source of general information, though it is always worth while making a direct approach to large hospitals. Part-time posts are seldom generally advertised, though they may appear on the cards in Jobcentres. If you are thinking of resuming work, it is a good idea to renew professional contacts and take a professional journal. Many part-time appointments are achieved through informal contacts.

Medicine

Medicine is a special case among the professions on several counts. First, the rate of development in medical practice makes it difficult to take a complete break away from work. Then, the long hours worked by doctors in the most junior posts (often 80-100 hours a week) are a virtually impossible undertaking for anyone with family responsibilities, yet it is in just these posts that part-time work is most scarce. Third, the prolonged process of postgraduate training, which is a requirement for everyone seeking a career as a specialist, was established with a largely male and full-time workforce in view. The profession has been slow to respond to the needs of women who demand both a career and a family life.

In the past, many women doctors who married and had children were lost to medicine altogether. Today, their counterparts often find themselves acting as an 'extra pair of hands' in medical and clinical assistant posts with no promotion prospects, because it is here that part-time work is most easily found. Before abhorring the situation and proceeding to consider the alternatives, it is worth while pausing to consider the contribution made to medicine by these so-called humble functions, because job satisfaction consists largely of feeling that a job is worth doing and you are able to do it well, whatever the other rewards. The professional hierarchy of medicine was created on the assumption that good medical practice is synonymous with academic excellence, but this view is now being challenged from some quarters. More importance is vested in the quality of the relationship between doctor and patient and the life experience and human understanding doctors can bring to their work. There is also a new emphasis on prevention rather than cure — of seeing medicine in a wider context than the (however brilliant) solving of medical conundrums once the disability has set in. Non-career posts operate on just these frontiers, in positions of day-to-day contact with patients and in the field of prevention, and part-timers are often ideally suited to fill them because they are, by definition, people who have freed themselves from the institutional mould by demanding more time for their personal selves.

Sessional Non-training Medical Work
This is usually associated with hospital work, but includes locum work in general practice and in community health clinics. For the doctor it can provide valuable experience through the contact with patients, and, for the patient, the sessional doctor can be the first contact with the medical profession in a particular institution. Locum work can lack continuity, but if sessions are undertaken with any regularity this should not be the case. Payment is by the session, and hours are reasonably flexible with the proviso that a complete session must be worked on each occasion. Such work does not, however, count towards promotion.

Community Health
Community health clinics are an important part of the primary care sector. They concentrate on prevention and deal mainly with women and their young families. They work in close association with the school doctor service and with local GPs.

Employment is on a sessional basis and part-timing is well established. This is the one area of medicine in which you can practise independently without undertaking postgraduate training, but its rating within the medical hierarchy is low. Promotion prospects are limited — there are just two grades of responsibility — and you will suffer the indignity of being unable to prescribe medicines, though you can supply contraceptives.

Part-time Postgraduate Training

Postgraduate training is mandatory for people wishing to enter hospital specialisation and community medicine, or to become a principal in general practice. This is particularly difficult for women, because training is most usually undertaken during the years when they are likely to be raising their families; it demands a certain amount of mobility, and it occurs when their husbands are likely to be mobile in pursuit of their own careers — especially if they, too, are doctors.

Finding a Job

Although the *British Medical Journal* is the standard source of advertisements for medical posts, many part-time posts are not advertised.

Hospital work remains the most competitive branch of medicine. Advertising of part-time hospital posts is largely informal, and this, coupled with the fact that schemes vary regionally, makes it necessary for the individual to be well-informed. Supernumerary posts must, of course, be created on your own initiative. Postgraduate Deans are asked by the DHSS to provide a link between women doctors and the employing authorities, and reliable information and advice on all part-time medical posts can be gained from the Medical Women's Federation who have, from the outset, been strong supporters of the need for part-time opportunities. The Council for Postgraduate Medical Education will also give advice. Part-time general practitioners must look to group practices for work. Single-handed appointments are made by the local Family Practitioner Committee and advertised in the *British Medical Journal*, but appointments to group practices are often made by invitation, especially when they concern part-timers. The importance of renewing contacts and of personal recommendations cannot be over-emphasised.

HOSPITAL SPECIALISATION

Until the late 1960s, part-time hospital training posts were virtually unknown. Then the DHSS began to issue a steady output of memoranda urging health authorities to create part-time training posts to counteract the labour wastage among women, but giving no clear guidelines as to how schemes should operate. Some authorities, notably the Oxford Regional Health

Authority (RHA) — which, significantly, has the only woman Regional Medical Officer in England and Wales — and the Lothian Health Board, set up schemes genuinely aiming to provide equality of opportunity, but, in most cases, part-time training has been restricted to shortage specialties. A survey of women doctors undertaken in 1976 (see B Beaumont 'Special provisions for women doctors to train and practise in medicine after graduation: a report of a survey', *Medical Education*, 1979) found that over 50 per cent of authorisations for part-time posts were in two specialties — anaesthetics and mental illness — and that some specialties, notably the surgical ones, were particularly resistant to part-time training.

The same survey, however, noted a remarkable ignorance among the doctors themselves about the schemes available. Ignorance was a feature even in those regions seeking most actively to promote part-time training.

In 1972, the Women Doctors' Retainer Scheme was introduced. Part-time training schemes are open to both men and women, although in practice virtually no men opt for them, but the retainer scheme is aimed specifically at women who are unable to undertake any regular work for a while. It is available in all branches of medicine and provides a structure for keeping in touch through a minimum number of training and work sessions each year, until you are able to resume work or training. As with part-time training, retainer schemes have been set up and pursued with varying degrees of enthusiasm and effectiveness by different health authorities.

In 1979, authorisation for part-time senior registrar posts became the responsibility of the DHSS in an attempt to establish more equality of opportunity for part-timers (see DHSS Circular PM[79]3). The scheme is advertised nationally each autumn and it has gone some way towards improving the competitiveness of part-timers seeking posts in a variety of specialties. There are, however, some anomalies. Authorisation is automatic in shortage specialties but not others, and funding is provided at regional level, so that it is possible to obtain DHSS approval for a training post, yet find that funding is not forthcoming locally.

There are three types of arrangement under which part-time training can be carried out: through appointment to a designated part-time post, through job-sharing a full-time establishment post, and in a supernumerary post.

Outside the scheme relating specifically to senior registrar posts the DHSS designates only a few part-time posts, and these do not meet the demands of women wishing to work part-time. None is available in surgical specialties in which the stated position is that part-time training can only be considered on merit in individual cases.

The second option, that of job-sharing, ought in theory to be available everywhere, but it has, so far, been confined to a few regions. Job-sharers must obtain a full-time post jointly in open competition, having first convinced the consultant that the arrangement is acceptable. Their contract of employment should define the division of their duties, and of employment benefits and remuneration. It should contain a clause protecting them in the eventuality of one partner leaving the post — the most usual arrangement is an offer of the full-time post or, if this is unacceptable, of a part-time supernumerary one.

Many people, however, are thrown back on supernumerary posts which they must set up for themselves. The process can be long and tortuous, occupying months and, sometimes, years. First, you must find a consultant willing to take you, then you must seek the approval of the relevant Royal College, and finally you must approach the DHSS for funding. Supernumerary posts have disadvantages beyond the difficulty involved in creating them. As they are not obtained in open competition they can be regarded with resentment by some colleagues, who consider that you have taken a side door into training. They are also outside the system which relates the number of training posts to the expected number of consultant vacancies and are therefore accepted reluctantly by many health authorities. There is general agreement that supernumerary training should be replaced by a greater flexibility within the established training network and that more centralised administration of funding for training posts would be welcome. (See a survey of regional health authorities commissioned by the King Edward Hospital Fund for London, 1980.)

The quality of training need not be inferior if your post is properly set up, though you may need to work harder to prove your worth and gain the acceptance of colleagues as part-timers commonly lack credibility. In this respect, job-sharers are at an advantage as, between them, they fill a full-time post and are not seen to be 'special cases' or in receipt of concessions. The prolongation of the training period — which is doubled if you work half-time — can be a rather daunting prospect, but for many people this is inevitable, as even a part-time post involves 40 or 50 hours of work each week — a heavy undertaking for someone with family responsibilities.

GENERAL PRACTICE

Not much information is available about part-time training posts in general practice, probably because mandatory training has only recently been introduced. DHSS memoranda have concentrated on the need for schemes to ease the return of women who have been away from work for a period, and refresher courses should, theoretically, be available.

People who need to undertake training (ie all those who were not already practising as a principal before August 1982) have two options: a package deal of hospital posts and trainee year in general practice, or a self-arranged combination of posts, including a trainee GP year, which fulfil the requirements of the Royal College of General Practitioners. Some part-time posts are available, but with the shorter training period (three years) it is likely that demand has not been strong enough to urge their creation on a significant scale. You may think it best to postpone your family until you have completed your training. If this is not possible, you must enter the same lists as hospital doctors in seeking a post. Each health authority has an adviser in general practice who, together with the postgraduate dean, should be able to help.

Once your training is behind you, you should find that general practice is easily adaptable to part-time work now that the trend is towards group practice. The quality of work will depend on the prevailing attitudes to part-timers in the practice where you work, and the extent to which you are able to maintain continuity in your treatment of patients. Although your surgery hours will be arranged by negotiation, you will need to be able to undertake your share of on-call duties. As remuneration is based on the number of patients on your list, and general practices have autonomy to arrange their financial affairs, your parity with full-timers will depend on the way in which the spoils are divided in your practice.

COMMUNITY MEDICINE

The training for community medicine runs parallel with that for hospital specialisation with the difference that part of it

149

involves a course of formal study, usually at registrar or senior registrar level. The 1979 DHSS Circular (PM[79]3) ruled that part-time posts at these grades should be created by the health authorities with the DHSS being notified of the appointments. People wishing to train in community medicine may be helped by the fact that a fairly high proportion of consultants are women and therefore likely to be sympathetic to their needs.

Dentistry

Prospects for the part-timer in dentistry are influenced by the facts that only a very small section of practice requires postgraduate training and that the rate of development in general dental practice is far slower than it is in medicine. On the other hand, dentistry is a craft skill which can grow rusty if left for too long. In 1979, the Dentists' Retainer Scheme was introduced to run along similar lines to the one in medicine, and this, together with some availability of refresher courses, provides a structure for easing your return to work if you give up for any length of time.

Finding a Job

Some jobs in general practice are advertised in the dental journals, but many more are filled through personal recommendation or previous contacts. For posts in hospital dentistry, see p 151. Part-time opportunities in community dentistry are good. It is worth contacting the Area Dental Officer, as there may be posts available which have not been advertised.

GENERAL PRACTICE

Eighty per cent of all dentists work in general practice for which there are currently no postgraduate training requirements. On the face of it, prospects for part-timers look good. General practice, with its tendency towards group practice, is well adapted to part-time work as there will always be another dentist available in an emergency. Also, the method of payment, for each item of work done, places part-timers on a level of equality with other colleagues, and is clearly defined.

General practices are run as small, independent businesses by the partners or principals and the exact terms of your employment will depend on your employer's attitude to part-timers. You will, most likely, be an associate, receiving a proportion of the fees you earn and contributing the rest to practice overheads. There is no evidence that you will be treated differently from full-timers in this respect.

As general practices must run on a profit basis, many dentists will be unwilling to see surgeries remaining unused, so you may find it difficult to persuade anyone to take you on for a shortened day unless the times you do not work can be filled by other part-timers. The easiest rota to arrange is one in which several dentists work for complete days — but the working day in dentistry can be long.

There are not the communication problems in dentistry that there are in other professions as the main channels of communication are between dentist and patient. You will have your own patients, and as emergencies are rare, job satisfaction should be little different from that experienced in full-time work.

THE COMMUNITY DENTAL SERVICE
The community dental service is, in many ways, ideal for the part-timer. Posts are salaried and most clinical work is done during school hours. The brief of the community dentist is wide, embracing public health matters as well as dentistry *per se*. Work is varied and much of it involves the treatment of children and elderly people.

HOSPITAL SPECIALISATION
People wishing to become hospital specialists must go through the same process as hospital doctors, with one important difference — there are no shortage specialties in dentistry. The field is therefore extremely competitive, with only a handful of posts available, whether full- or part-time. If you are really determined, you may have to pioneer your own part-time training, with the help, perhaps, of a consultant sympathetic to your aims.

CASE STUDIES

Mary. Hospital Nurse
Mary has worked part-time on the same children's intensive care ward for 12 years. She has two sons aged 13 and 10.

'I am afraid I am untypical because no one would get a job like mine today. When I started, there was a nursing shortage and hospitals were willing to be flexible over hours, but today they abide by the rules. I work regular hours — 9.00 am to 2.00 pm — and I take the school holidays off as unpaid leave. This was only possible because there was an experienced ward sister who had the confidence to press for unorthodox arrangements. Also, I had previous experience as a sister on

151

an intensive care ward, and that helped. I am a staff nurse now. Part-timers cannot be sisters.

I chose my hospital because it was one of the few with a nursery, and initially I worked for the satisfaction of it. Since then my husband has been made redundant and has taken a lower paid job, so now we need the money. I still take the school holidays off, but often I do a couple of nights a week instead, to make up for the lost income.

You are a general dogsbody basically, when you work the sort of hours I do. When I arrive everybody else has already been working for an hour, so I don't get any total patient care. So I'm not really kept in touch, and to this extent it is less satisfying. I do all the odd jobs. I always do the drugs round and a whole range of things no one but me ever does. No decisions were made. It just grew up over the years — mainly, I think, because I felt guilty about my convenient hours and tended to take on all the things people disliked, to compensate.

The hospital has been very good to me. I have never been pressed to take on emergency work, and they have accommodated me when my children were ill. I think they value my contribution on a children's ward because I am a parent and I *know* how the mothers are feeling in the situations they encounter.

I think the reduction in the employment of part-timers is a great shame. There were seven on my ward when I started and now I am the only one. The tragic thing is that we use so many agency nurses when there are many people who would jump at the chance of a permanent part-time appointment if the hours were more flexible. I know a number of the married girls who would like to cut down on their hours, but they can't. I agree we need rules, but allowances should be made in areas where more flexibility is possible.'

Josie. Dental Surgery Assistant

Josie works for 10 hours a week for a large group practice employing five full-time dentists and a number of specialists on a part-time basis. She is divorced and has two children aged 8 and 10.

'I have worked for the same practice, full- and part-time, for 17 years. I worked part-time for a while after the children were born, but then my husband was made redundant, so the children went to an all-day nursery and I returned to full-time work. When they started school I had to cut down my hours so that I could collect them, so I worked mornings only, splitting the day with another girl.

When she left, I was offered the full-time job. But I ruled it out for two reasons: first, I had recently divorced and I felt it would not be good for the kids; second, as a single parent on a low income, I get various allowances. If I had gone full-time and paid for child-minding, I would have been worse off.

So I asked to continue part-time but all they could offer me was one evening a week from 6.00 to 9.00 pm and all day Saturday. In fact, this suits me quite well as my ex-husband has the children at weekends and it gets me out. But if I had the choice, I would like to be here more often and keep track of what's going on. Ideally, I would like to work every day from 9.30 am to 3.30 pm, but they can't give me more hours on a regular basis. I do work, though, when anybody's off sick or on holiday. It's irregular, and often I get no warning, but it gives me higher earnings on average. I always try to take the work I'm offered, because I think that if I turn it down the opportunity may not arise again. I bend over backwards to accommodate my employers, but by the same token they are very understanding about my problems. If there's a sudden emergency with the children, there's no question — I go! I have even brought them into work with me on occasions, but that's not ideal.

I get the same rate of pay as full-timers, but no sick pay or paid holidays. When I was full-time and had to have time off for the kids I was paid, but now I'm only paid for the hours I actually do. Even if I leave unexpectedly during the day, it is deducted from my pay. I work with different dentists. If you've got your own dentist you know where everything is and you take a pride in the surgery. Now, it can be annoying not finding things, but I still enjoy it very much.

Dentistry has changed a great deal since I started working. In those days we had gas sessions — we used to call them 'Bloody Fridays'! — when we would shove a gas mask over faces and all the teeth would be taken out. We did, maybe, 16 patients in the hour before lunch. It horrifies me to remember it. Now, we have a highly qualified anaesthetist and it's quite a performance. She gives the patients a thorough physical examination beforehand and monitors their recovery afterwards. I like working with her. I also like it when I get in with the orthodontist and the oral surgeon. It's much more interesting than routine fillings and X-rays, and one of the advantages of working in a large practice.'

Margaret. Physiotherapist and Ante-natal Teacher
Margaret has two small children and has tried, and rejected, combining motherhood with full-time work.

'I began doing the Natural Childbirth Trust (NCT) course in ante-natal teaching after the birth of my second child and I did it with a long-term view. Part-time posts in physiotherapy are becoming scarcer with the expenditure cuts, and their hours can be very rigid. I thought I would have more choice if I had a speciality, so now, with my NCT training behind me, I am working for my membership of the obstetrics and gynaecology section of the Royal College of Physiotherapists.

I found the whole business of having babies frightfully interesting — seeing it from the other side — and I felt that I could use my skills to make the system better. I had the experience of a year of full-time work when my first child was four, and I found it absolutely exhausting. I worked on an intensive care unit and it was emotionally and physically draining so that I found it hard to give my child enough of me and of my time. Then I became pregnant again. It was unintentional but a blessing in disguise because it forced me to look for alternatives.

My husband works on oil rigs and it can be dangerous, so I wanted to make sure that if I was left alone I'd have enough money to survive. Behind my need to keep in with my work skills is the feeling that I am

153

the person who could be left with all the responsibility. So I began taking the NCT course because it was something I could do with a young baby. You can work at your own pace and the NCT are very understanding about family problems.

So far, I've restricted myself to a few hours' commitment each week, taking ante-natal classes in my house. It is very nice working from home because I can always see people if they want to talk. I have the time to be flexible in this way. With mothers and babies, the follow-up is equally important, and though I'm not paid for it, it's something I do. I feel very strongly that women need and should get support. After my first child I was very depressed. I viewed myself as a professional woman and, suddenly, I felt I had nothing. It was a problem of identity. So my work is a matter of conviction as much as practicality. I hope I will be in a position to build up my commitment as the children get older, but I'm also laying the foundation for making it the kind of work I believe in and want to do.'

Sylvia. Ante-natal Teacher

The break in her working life caused by the arrival of her children prompted Sylvia to change tack. She is now establishing herself in a completely different line of work.

'I haven't got a profession *per se*. I trained as a secretary, but I've done lots of things. If you are lucky, doors do open out of secretarial training. The best job I had (full-time, of course) was as an assistant account executive in an advertising agency. I handled the clients and presented the campaigns to them.

Then I got married and had four children. The youngest is nearly six. For a time after the first baby I did temping — working one week on and one off. I combined with a friend and we swapped babies. Later, I became a permanent temporary through a contact I made in one of my jobs, working one day a week in the same firm, and that suited me fine. But after the birth of my second child I stopped working altogether.

When number four was growing up I started looking around and thinking — where am I going? I decided that I didn't want to return to pounding a typewriter in some grotty office — financially, there's not much in it if you only work part-time, when you consider the costs of child-minding, a few decent clothes and fast foods to help you cope. But work does other things for you. It relieves the pressure of the domestic scene. You're away from it all and you realise you are a person.

I toyed with the idea of taking further training, but to do it with least pain it has to be full-time. And with four children and a house and husband to look after, this was impossible. I would really like to have done a midwifery course because I was so horrified at the treatment I got when I was having my third child — I wanted to work from the inside and change the world! But my husband said there was no way in which I could manage it. So, as second best, I chose to work from the other side and do ante-natal teaching.

THE HEALTH CARE PROFESSIONS

I began as a breast-feeding counsellor five years ago. It's a very simple thing — more like a hobby — and doesn't take up much time. Then I did the Natural Childbirth Trust course which I have recently finished. The useful aspect is that you teach at times which suit. I do no evening teaching, for instance, though this does rule out teaching couples, which is the big thing now. But my husband travels a lot, so I can't rely on him to help with the children in the evenings. People get referred to me by the NCT and they pay their course fee — at the moment it's £20 for eight lessons — direct to me.* There's not a lot of money in it, but I find it very satisfying. I take groups of about five at a time, and maybe I teach twice or three times a week. I couldn't do too much of this kind of teaching anyway, because it's an emotional involvement as well. It shouldn't overwhelm you, but emotional support is part of the service that you give.

The NCT is largely a middle class movement and I am very keen on teaching women who wouldn't normally come. I've begun a class in a local hall, just charging a nominal amount to cover the cost of the hall. I leafleted the nearby estates and though I only got three women, two of them would definitely not otherwise have gone to ante-natal classes, so I feel very pleased. I'm planning to contact local doctors' surgeries and see if they can alert any women they know who are not going to hospital classes.

I'm very anti drugs and I'm having success. Most of the women from my classes have managed to refuse them — though there are times when drugs are necessary. I'm not totally against intervention; only against it when it is inessential. But I'm hopeful — I think the mood is changing.

I made the right decision. I'm loving the work. The only thing I regret is that I don't work away from home. I would like the stimulus of going out, and would like to keep my work and home life separate.'

Christine. A Hospital Doctor

Christine is employed by the Lothian Health Board. She has been job-sharing for three years in a post as senior registrar in obstetrics and gynaecology.

'Obstetrics and gynaecology is a very demanding branch of medicine in terms of work load, on call commitments and so forth. It is a particularly suitable specialty for women, yet there are very few women consultants in it. This is probably because of the difficulty of completing the training requirements at a time when most women are having their children — you don't usually become eligible for consultant posts until at least the age of 35.

Provision can theoretically be made for a woman doctor to continue her training in supernumary, part-time posts, but such posts lack credibility with colleagues and create ill-feeling because 'special arrangements' are being made. In hospital medicine, job-sharing is a much better arrangement. It maintains the *status quo* and gives the sharers a well-defined role as they are, together, filling a 'complete' post. It

* This was in 1983.

has certainly enabled me to combine family life with pursuing my career in my chosen branch of medicine.

The background to my shared post is that a vacancy at the appropriate grade came up in the hospital where I and my present job partner had been working for some time. We had both completed our training up to that point in full-time posts and were both pregnant for the first time. We competed for the post on the open market and applied jointly, with some trepidation, as such an arrangement had never occurred before in our specialty, although it had worked well in other branches of medicine in the region. We were met with varying reactions from our colleagues, but had the support of some of the more senior consultants – and got the job!

In any job where co-operation is needed, the choice of job partner is very important. We had to ensure, for instance, that our ideas on patient care were compatible. We can maintain a degree of independence in elective work and outpatient clinics but all emergency work and on-call duties must be shared. We have to be very organised and all routine work must be distributed equally between us because we have certain training requirements to fulfil. In many practical ways there have been positive benefits. We have always covered each other's leave and, in this way, we have each had a second child without losing any training accreditation or causing any inconvenience to our colleagues.

Of course there are problems – actual and potential. We both work considerably in excess of our contracted hours, yet as we are considered to work half-time, we will have to complete double the number of years to gain full recognition. We have both found that our spells of full-time duty covering each other's leave gave us greater job satisfaction, although they had the disadvantage of causing some behavioural problems in our children and complaints that our spouses never saw us! But, in general, we find the shared post creates considerable job satisfaction and we still have enough energy left over to carry on with some research and to spend time at home with the family.

My children are now three-and-a-half and seven months old. I have always employed a live-in housekeeper/mother's help to lessen my domestic chores and to ensure that someone is in the house if I am called out. My husband is also a hospital doctor, with long and irregular working hours. Both children spend part of the day at a playcentre run for the children of hospital staff, but I couldn't rely on this alone. I pay a great deal of money in child-care, so feel little financial benefit from working. I feel that working women in my position should be eligible for some tax concessions on this account.

I look upon my job-sharing as a temporary arrangement. When I have completed my training, and my children are older, I shall look for a full-time consultant post. It will not be easy, because I will be restricted geographically by the interests of my husband's career, but at least consultant work, although carrying more responsibility, is less demanding than it is at junior grades. In the meanwhile, I feel that job-sharing has proved the ideal solution for me, but I am also aware that I was fortunate and the situation might have been very different.'

Liz. Dental Surgeon

Liz works part-time in general practice. She has three children aged 10, 8 and 4½

'I have worked for the same practice full- and part-time for 15 years, and the longest I've been away is a little over three months.

I began my part-time work with a day and a half after the birth of my first child. Although I was known at the practice as a good and reliable worker I was offered no concessions, so I realised that if I wanted to work school hours I would have to work in a school clinic. I didn't want to do this, so I accepted the terms I was given. On my full day I worked from 9.30 am until 6.00 pm, and on my half day from 9.30 am until 1.00 pm. I used relations to look after the baby. It was not always easy.

After the birth of my second child, I employed someone to look after the children for a while, and later I did a swap with two friends and that worked very well. Now, I work for two mornings and one full day, and I employ a 'demi-pair' while I'm away to do light housework and look after the children if they are ill.

I am an associate at the practice and get paid 50 per cent of what I earn. I think this is the most usual arrangement for full-timers too.

I have never taken time off for the children, yet I know that employers are prejudiced against women with children precisely on that score. They fear absenteeism more than anything. There was another part-time job going at our practice and a very nice woman with two children turned up for it. My boss liked her, but in the end he employed a man because he was afraid her children would make her less dependable. At that time, he had employed me for 15 years — 10 of them part-time — and I have had less time off than the men!

As a dentist, I think you can afford to cope with your children, if need be, by employing an *au pair*. You do not need to be unreliable. Admittedly, I've been lucky. I found good friends; my kids did not have the contagious diseases; and my husband is self-employed, so he can step in in an emergency. Even so, I don't want to work full-time. It would be too difficult because I like to see my children after school. I do extra hours if anyone is away, but then I'm doing a favour and I can choose the hours. Maybe my boss would give me a shortened day if I worked every day — because he knows that I'm reliable — but what would I do during the school holidays?'

Chapter 10

Other Professional Work

Introduction

In some professions, permanent part-time work is almost impossible to find; in one or two, opportunities are good. This difference is not only governed by the nature of the job — the extent of its adaptability to part-time working — it also depends on the strength of female representation within the profession concerned. The concentration of women in just a few occupations across the whole field of employment is repeated in microcosm in the professions. Women are to be found in education, the social sciences, the welfare sector and in work of a (loosely) literary nature, but only 4 per cent of architects, 7 per cent of barristers and 0.5 per cent of engineers are women. In these professions, male interests prevail and no concessions are made to women's domestic commitments, or, indeed, to the wishes of the few men who might like to step out of line and work part-time.

Terms and Conditions of Work

It is difficult to generalise about the quality of part-time work, except to say that women, generally, do badly in the professions and part-timers do worst of all.

Lack of promotion prospects is a common feature of part-timing in most professions. Although a part-time contribution is often valued at the highest levels, and specialist consultants can spread their favours over several organisations, the middle ground is usually occupied solely by full-time staff, and part-timers are employed only in the lowest grades. Many will be women who previously held more responsible posts full-time, because professional women tend to have their families later, after they have established their careers. They will therefore be experiencing not only a loss of status but a drop in pay, *pro rata*. Although most professions pay part-time staff at the full-time rate, this is, of course, the rate for the grade in which they are employed.

One drawback to the promotion of part-timers is the fact that many higher grade posts involve administrative duties or the management of other staff. It is easier to promote on grounds of ability and experience in jobs which can be divided into self-contained workloads than in situations where promotion involves additional functions which it is assumed a part-timer cannot perform. Yet, in relation to the size of the problem (women form half of the working population, though not all of them are able to be active at any one time, and most spend some time out of work and/or work part-time when they have children), little real attempt has been made to find solutions. Job-sharing offers the most constructive way forward, but it is, as yet, a minority arrangement and looked upon by most employers with distrust, caution or disinterest. Most professions are competitive enough under the present arrangements. They do not need to make allowances for part-timers.

Significantly enough, when initiatives are taken, they arouse the interest of men as well as women, suggesting that the prevailing inflexibility in career paths is not welcomed by all men — they merely find it easier to conform to it. To quote an example, the acceptance of job-sharing as a policy by local government has prompted a few highly placed male officers to consider the possibility of combining professional life with academic research. If more men, especially those in influential positions, join the part-time lobby, its strength will be greatly increased.

However, moves to improve the conditions of part-time work come mainly from women. Under the leadership of a woman, the Inner London Education Authority sponsors research into why London's women teachers do so badly in career terms. One of the questions posed in an attempt to establish a framework for the research was, 'Would it help if part-time teachers could be appointed to posts above Scale 1?' It is obvious that it would, and it was important that the question had been asked. Any examination of women's poor career performance must give due consideration to the forfeit they pay during their childbearing years. In most working situations, career continuity cannot be maintained except through full-time work. This means that many women have two careers, not one: before, and after, their children. For a while they mark time, or backslide, and then they begin again.

In this situation, most people regard their part-timing as a temporary arrangement, and this is also how it is seen by employers. It is harder for part-time workers to secure permanent contracts, though their temporary contracts will, admittedly, deal more generously with them in terms of employment-related benefits than is usually the case with their non-professional counterparts. In some professions, part-timers may be confined mainly to locum work; in others, freelancing might be the most satisfactory arrangement. Each has its advantages and disadvantages and will be influenced, not least, by the individual's expectations of the rewards of work.

An examination of the prevailing conditions in each profession is beyond the scope of this book. The following examples have been chosen because they are fairly representative of the spread of opportunities in different occupations, or because they describe working arrangements which might be useful to know about. In many cases, part-timers will have to carve out their own career paths by instigating working situations which are not the norm — unless they meet with a rigid career structure which prevents them from doing so.

Law

Men in the law consider that women in the profession are tough. They have to be, because they are contending in a highly competitive male profession. Even so, they have not been too successful in establishing part-time opportunities.

The law changes, and this poses problems for anyone who has taken some time away from work. Even if you have, through your own efforts, kept abreast of new developments, you may have some difficulty in convincing potential employers of this. The assumption will be that your knowledge is out of date and you will therefore be a less cost-effective person.

Finding a Job
Locum work can be obtained through legal agencies, and The Law Society has a register of vacancies. Job advertisements appear in *The Times* on Tuesdays, in the *Law Society Gazette*, and occasionally, for posts in community law, in the *Guardian* on Wednesdays and in *New Society*. You can always advertise, yourself, but if you want a permanent appointment you are well advised to resume contact with previous colleagues and employers.

Solicitors

PRIVATE PRACTICE

Women are entering private practice in greater numbers and are even becoming partners — but on a full-time basis. Part-time opportunities are confined mainly to locum work, most often in the summer months, and occasionally to short-term contracts, helping out with large cases. There is, therefore, a confusion between part-time and temporary opportunities. Now and again, solicitors may need an extra three days' help weekly on a permanent basis but usually they will fill these posts by invitation, asking a previous colleague to return part-time. Most part-time work is associated with conveyancing.

Private practice provides a service to the public and high standards must be maintained, including an immediate response to all situations and queries. For this reason, part-time work is quite difficult to arrange, especially in litigation. The practical problems are not as great in conveyancing.

THE VOLUNTARY SECTOR

Attitudes to part-timers are more sympathetic in the voluntary sector. Community Law Centres employ solicitors part-time, mainly to deal with housing problems and other issues arising from the individuals' relationship with bureaucracy. Though the work may be rewarding, remuneration will usually be lower than in private practice. Citizens' Advice Bureaux also use solicitors, but services are often given on a voluntary basis.

THE BAR

Some barristers are employed by organisations but most are self-employed and therefore able to regulate the amount of work they do. It may be difficult to ensure an even flow of work and, to this extent, being a barrister always involves some periods of part-time work. For the person with other commitments it will be a case of dovetailing conflicting demands and maintaining enough of a presence to preserve a foothold in a very competitive world. When you are working you must be able to be on the spot, though you may have slacker periods in between.

At one time, it was quite rare for women to become barristers but, today, there are more women at the bar and, of these, many have young children and are coping well. As a self-employed person you cannot be discriminated against professionally on the grounds that your commitment is part-time.

Teaching

Comparatively few school teachers work part-time, probably because the short hours of the school day enable more women to take on a full-time commitment. Part-timing is only established, therefore, as a fringe activity, where timetabling requirements make it expedient.

Most authorities only employ part-timers in Scale 1 posts, often on a supply, or temporary terminal basis. This means that part-time teaching is an insecure form of employment outside the career structure of the profession as a whole. Apart from this, part-time teachers have identical terms of employment, *pro rata*, with full-timers, though they must make a special request to be included in the superannuation scheme. As this point is made in very small print on the contract of employment, it can easily be missed!

Recently, there has been an interest in the condition of part-time work among teachers themselves, and moves have been made to counteract the disadvantages, which have met with a response from some authorities. Job-sharing has been introduced, though in small numbers, as a way of overcoming the barrier to part-timers gaining promotion. The arrangement, unfortunately, poses a problem which is not encountered elsewhere. Although it is an accepted fact that teachers work far longer than their specified hours, legally they are only employed during them. A teacher must work for more than five sessions out of 10 each week to total 16 hours and qualify for protection under employment law, and this is not possible for job-sharers. What is needed is an additional commitment on the part of the employer to compensate for loss of protection in law. This fact, incidentally, means that proportionately more part-time teachers are unprotected than is the case for part-timers in other occupations.

The quality of part-time work is dependent on the lines of communication operating at any one time. A large part of the job remains intact, because it involves direct communication between teacher and pupils — though children are quick to detect the 'hierarchy' and infer that part-timers are at the bottom of the pile. But communication with colleagues is another matter. It is easy to be left out because you are not on site at the right time, or, quite simply, you are not regarded as a person worth consulting, or wishing to be involved.

Another form of work open to the part-time teacher is home tutoring. It can be convenient, challenging, and, in itself, rewarding but it is the poor relation of the teaching profession. Salaries are low and paid only for the hours you actually work, which will depend not only on your wishes but on the demand for your services. Your name will be placed on the panel of home tutors in the area in which you wish to work and you will be called upon when needed. You will not get paid holidays or sick pay, and if you work more than a certain number of hours, your hourly pay rate is lowered.

Most children in need of home tutoring are temporarily out of school because of personal problems. Bad behaviour, truanting and pregnancy are the commonest reasons. The role of the home tutor is to form a constructive relationship with each child which will lead to his or her return to school, and to make up for loss of education in the meanwhile. It is an important job, but one which is scandalously unacknowledged.

It is also possible to work in adult and further education on a sessional, part-time basis. Hourly pay rates may seem fairly attractive (for instance, in Inner London, adult education tutors were paid £9.61 an hour in 1986), but there is no provision for pay during the holiday periods, or for other benefits enjoyed by full-time staff.

Finding a Job
Part-time posts are often filled informally in the first instance. If this is not possible, advertising is through the bulletin of the local authority concerned, and rarely in the national press or educational journals. Once again, the usefulness of previous contacts must be stressed. Vacancies on home tutoring pa.iels are not usually advertised. You should apply direct to your local education authority for inclusion on the panel.

Indexing

Indexing is one of several occupations connected with publishing, most of which can be undertaken on a freelance basis. Much indexing is carried out by freelancers and it is one of the more readily available forms of work, once you have made your contacts. Standards are high, and the work is hard, so it should not be thought of as an easy way of making money.

Although general subject indexing is available (cookery books, annuals, etc), most work requires a specialist knowledge of the subject concerned, so it will help if you can offer knowledge in a particular field.

Many people come to indexing via writing, publishing and librarianship but there is no reason why people from other professional backgrounds should not do the work. The Rapid Results College (see Part 3, p 188) has a correspondence course which gives a thorough grounding in all aspects of indexing, and, unless you are already experienced, the course is an essential prerequisite to taking on work.

Indexing requires disciplined thinking and can be a rewarding mental occupation. There is little acknowledgement for your hard work, however, as you will seldom receive any comment from your employers, or mention of your name in the publication. As with many forms of freelance work, you work in isolation.

Professional standards and conditions of work are maintained by the Society of Indexers. It is worth while taking out membership, as your name will be sent out in a list to publishers indicating the subjects in which you specialise. The Society also maintains a register of indexers, but standards for inclusion in the register are fairly stringent and you must already have some experience of the work before you apply. The Society acts as a liaison between registered members and publishers so there are obvious advantages in becoming registered.

Officially, payment is on an hourly basis. This seems fair as some jobs are more difficult and therefore more time-consuming than others, but it can present problems if you become skilled and very fast at the work.

Finding Work

The best way of getting started is through personal contacts. Without these, you can write to 50 publishers and find that they have no work to offer you at the time. Probably the highest paid form of work is journal indexing and it has the advantage of providing a regular flow of work. It is better to work as much as possible for one employer because you will receive better treatment all round.

Social Work

Part-time opportunities are good in social work although availability will vary according to the employer's attitude

and commitment to this form of employment. The best opportunities will be found with those authorities or organisations
known to employ a high proportion of part-timers. Overall,
there is probably more competition for part-time posts than
there used to be, as the increase in the number of men in the
profession has brought about an increase in the number of
posts which can be filled by full-timers.

Part-time workers are less discriminated against than they
are in other professions for two reasons. First, the career
structure is relatively simple as there are only three levels of
promotion and part-time posts are available in all three; second,
as jobs divide into case loads, all have a reasonable degree of
autonomy and do not lend themselves to the designation of
'subsidiary' roles as is the case in other occupations. Probably
because the distinctions between full- and part-time work are
blurred, there are also no clear differences in terms of employment. Part-timers have full parity, *pro rata*, with full-time
colleagues, but there are, however, aspects of the work and
benefits which are not to their advantage.

Disadvantages relate to workloads. If you work overtime the
rule is that you take time off in lieu. As part-timers tend to get
proportionately heavier case loads, they are *more* likely to work
beyond their hours, but *less* likely ever to find the time to
repay themselves in the routine manner. This is a Catch 22
situation for which there is, at present, no solution.

Pressure of work is a major influence in other ways, too.
It is more difficult for a part-timer to take on such tasks as the
supervision of students, and more essential to keep up to date
with paperwork in case colleagues should need to consult your
files in your absence. It is normal for part-timers to work
through their lunch hours, and they have less time available for
systems of professional support and other re-stoking processes
which can be so necessary in a stressful occupation.

The pressure is greatest in the social services departments
of local authorities. Nine out of 10 appointments are at clients'
homes, involving a time loss during travelling. There is a high
rate of emergencies — of non-accidental injury, of care orders,
etc — and this, coupled with exposure to the critical glare of the
media and public opinion generally, puts tremendous pressure
on all workers. Part-timers suffer most of all because they have
to be absent for longer periods from situations which cannot
comfortably be left, and, all too often, the only solution is to
work beyond set hours. Social services work is not containable,

165

but it must be exerienced by all workers as at least two years of 'generic' social work is a prerequisite for promotion.

Working for other agencies — for example, hospitals or child guidance clinics — is rather less of a scramble. Most appointments are at the workplace and work is not done in an atmosphere of constant crisis. In hospitals you have the assurance of knowing that your clients are in a protected situation during your absence, and this makes the work more possible on a part-time basis. There are fewer urgent calls upon you, and though you will probably have a heavy case load you have a greater measure of control.

Community Work

Community work is an offshoot of social work, a development of more radical thought and practice. Though opportunities are numerically less, they may be wider in their scope and offer a variety of working arrangements, demonstrating the ideals behind the work itself. It would be a contradiction for any distinctions to be made between one worker and another, so, on the face of it, community work is an ideal setting in which part-timers may expect to work on equal terms with their full-time colleagues.

Finding a Job
Professional journals, *New Society*, the *Guardian* on Wednesdays, and sometimes the local press, carry job advertisements. Most part-time posts are advertised, and appointments made in the normal way for all jobs.

CASE STUDIES

Joanna. Secondary School Teacher
Joanna has two children aged 8 and 10. For two years she taught part-time, two-and-a-half days a week.

'I was head of a department for eight years before the birth of my first child and when I left, I blithely thought I would be welcomed back with open arms when I was ready to return. I stayed away for another eight years, which was a marvellous time for me, but obviously disastrous for my career.

I went back to the same school, working with a friend who had taken over my job when I had left. It was the best situation I could have found because we work well together and agree in our approach to teaching, but even so it was difficult. I felt so different, both because *I* had changed during the time away, and because the school, and my position in it, had changed. The people who remembered me were

166

friendly, but they always asked me how the children were, and didn't seem to think I would be interested in school matters any more. I was a sideline, as far as all that was concerned. I arrived, took my classes, and left.

I felt different with my pupils as well. After eight years of relating to children in an informal, family way, I found it hard to assume an authoritarian role and winced when I witnessed other teachers verbally gunning down offenders. There are certain ploys teachers use when talking to children, to manipulate them, and I had lost the skill. It seemed distasteful, too, because it is all an act and therefore basically dishonest. The trouble is that children are used to this treatment, and if you do not provide it it is harder to make them understand where the controls and barriers are. For a time I felt determined to win through to good relationships on a person-to-person basis, but gradually I began to adopt the more traditional role.'

Drusilla. Indexer

Drusilla has been a freelance indexer for 11 years. She has three children aged 10, 7 and 2.

'I did a course in librarianship, and while I was doing it a week's course in indexing was offered. I vaguely thought it might be useful in the future to be able to work at home, so I went on it. It was all rather basic (this was in the days before the correspondence course which is much more comprehensive) but it put me in touch with people from the Society of Indexers — including the man who gave me my start. He contacted me a while later and offered me some work on a law journal. He said he would teach me, and at the end of it I could become registered. By this time I was at home with a young baby and very much at a loose end, so I accepted his offer. Three months later he died, so that was an end to it, but in the meanwhile I had learned quite a lot of the mechanics of the job.

My next commission was the result of sheer nepotism — a medical manuscript obtained through the hospital where my husband worked as a doctor. I worked my way through it — *very* slowly — and after that I was given more work direct from the publisher.

Most of my commissions are medical ones. In a sense, indexing is a sort of game. I think it appeals to people who like playing games. And medical indexing is more tricky than most because the terminology is changing constantly. I enjoy the process. It's both absorbing and satisfying, because it is a self-contained problem which *you* resolve. But it is not something to be undertaken lightly on a nice steady two-hours-a-day basis. When work comes, there is usually an urgent deadline and you have to be prepared to drop everything to get it finished. The most difficult thing is deciding what to leave out. My method is to begin with everything and then cut it down until I reach the length limit.

A year-and-a-half ago, we bought a computer. My husband wanted it and he offered as justification the promise of writing me a program for indexing. Since then, I've been more involved with the mechanics than with the indexing itself — writing and re-writing programs which can run on a wide range of computers. It has been an interesting departure and has cut down on working time enormously.'

Sue. Freelance Copy Editor and Indexer

Sue has three children aged 9, 7 and 5 and, before they were born, she was an editor with a prestigious publishing house. Most of her freelance work is for her old employer.

'I've been freelancing for eight years now, working at home. When I gave up full-time employment, the publishers kept feeding me, so that I always had enough to do. It worked well until the birth of my third child which was a hiatus that made a tremendous difference. I had three children under five, and I found I couldn't cope.

All the boys are at school now, so I have climbed out of the trough and I have been able to increase my workload. The trouble is in my working situation itself. Editing is part of an ongoing situation from manuscript to printed book and I never see the other stages. I feel very cut off. I have nothing to measure myself against. No one tells me if I've done a good or a bad job. Some jobs are very large and I may live with them for months. Then — nothing. I have no involvement with the excitement and rewards of the finished product.

Recently, I've had a manuscript where the author has challenged my editing and it has made me wonder if I am over-correcting because I have lost my perspective. I know I'm getting stale and I need to get back into a social working situation.

Money is uneven because the flow of work is uneven, but a more annoying aspect of being freelance is that people don't pay you for such a long time. And when it comes, it's such a footling sum. I am paid for the time each job takes, and I get between £3.50 and £4.80 an hour.* I know I tend to underestimate the time I spend working.

From my point of view, I cannot convince myself that I am working. If people ask, "Do you work?" I say, "No". It's a question of my self-image and I'm only just realising that I must stop apologising for what I am. I'd love to have a label, but that's a much larger problem!

So far, I've always come just below the limit for paying income tax and I have no benefits except through my husband. I've never done freelance work flat out as a financially self-supporting job. My primary motive has been to keep myself intellectually involved.'

Hilary. Freelance Journalist

Hilary has two children aged 4 and 1. She writes features articles for newspapers and women's magazines.

'Apart from two short spells on the staff of magazines, I have been freelancing all my working life — for 12 years — and I reduced to a part-time commitment when my first daughter was born.

Being freelance before the children were born was a great advantage because I was already used to working at home so I only had one change to adapt to. I escaped the sense of isolation many women feel when they find themselves suddenly at home. I also found that, because

* This was in 1983.

the children would sleep for two hours at a stretch, I was more disciplined than before and used these times for working. These days, I work for two hours every morning and again in the evenings, depending on the work I have to do. The trouble is that it is uneven. I seem to have either three articles to write, or none at all. But when things go well, I think freelancing and motherhood are the perfect combination.

I got into freelance journalism by a mixture of luck and, I suppose, my own brazenness. While I was a student, I went to India (it was the time of the great "hippy" trail) and before I left I went round all the newspaper offices asking to see the editor. I got to see the Deputy Foreign Editor of one paper and asked him if he would be interested in some articles. Maybe he was impressed by my temerity, because he asked me to come back when I had written them. He liked the articles I wrote and though, in the event, they were never published, he put me on to other people who gave me my start.

You have to be motivated to freelance with a great deal of satisfaction. My past record is quite impressive, but I can't rest on my laurels. I have to keep on convincing people of what I can do. There's an old adage that you are only as good as the last thing you wrote.

There are attitudes, too, to overcome. I was once asked if I would be freelancing if I wasn't married — as if I was doing it for pin-money or as a hobby. Journalists can't make up their minds if they envy freelancers or loathe them. But the imagined freedom is largely illusory: we write what we are asked. And you need to have an awful lot of nerve, even if you are not a confident person, to push yourself and, sometimes, to press for payment afterwards.

There is a terrific amount of mobility these days in staff positions in journalism, and, as a freelancer, one is totally dependent on the prevailing mood. Even big names cannot feel secure. But I think I mind about this less now than I did. My life is divided into three areas: work, the children, and my union activities, and I cannot worry too much about any one of them.'

Jane. Social Worker

Jane works for a hospital in a Level 3 appointment, working 21 hours a week. She has three children aged 18, 13 and 8.

'I think I've been fortunate — maybe I'm not typical. In England I have never worked full-time, and have never lacked work.

What does make an enormous difference is where you trained. If you've been to a high status place, this counts for a lot. It certainly gets you an interview, though I'm sure that from then on the candidates are selected on merit. I went to the London School of Economics and did a course, which was not the best course going, but we had the "names" and it has proved a password!

Immediately after my degree I went to the States, and for eight years I worked full-time in a medical centre and in child guidance. When we returned, I had my third child and I did not work for three years. I was acclimatising. By that time, it was necessary to have a Certificate of Qualification in Social Work, so I did the London University extended course, which was excellent, and then went straight into a part-time job with a local authority. I stayed for two years and it

169

was a *long* two years. I learnt a lot but I was out until 11.00 pm — *and* I wasn't an inexperienced social worker who didn't know where the controls and boundaries were. I just had too much work.

Then I decided to do what I wanted and specialise. I decided that hospital work would be best for me. This was a very personal decision. For various reasons I intended to continue to work part-time, and I knew the hours would be more containable.

I have been in the job a year now, and my decision has been the right one. I have better supervision than I did with the local authority and there is more time for professional growth. It is built into the job rather than being considered a luxury only rarely available. I am now Level 3 — a working senior, but without administrative responsibilities. Level 3 workers supervise students, but this is difficult for part-timers because of the extra pressures upon them. I have almost the same number of cases as my full-time colleagues, although I work for 21 hours instead of 36. The pressures come from yourself, too. Part-timers are almost always too conscientious, maybe because they abandon the scene when others are still working.

If I had my time again, I would not have worked when the children were young. I can only say this because I am no longer the person I was then. When I was young I needed to prove myself, but now I am more at ease. I think I missed a great deal of my children and I can see the differences between my youngest child, who has had me at home, and the older two. They were always with babysitters and childminders, and I was negotiating my way around a complexity of arrangements. My eldest son sometimes didn't know who would meet him from school from one day to the next. A job can wait, but you can never recapture the years lost in your children's lives. If you work, I think that if anything suffers it is the family and not the job. That is why I have decided — at this late stage — to continue working part-time.'

Margie. Community Worker

Margie is one of four job-sharing workers running a small employment project. Her children are aged 7 and 9.

'My first experience of job-sharing was in my previous job, a project based on the East End of London. I job-shared with a friend and we were the only two part-timers. We had children of about the same ages and we swapped them around. That way, one of us was able to get to all the meetings and report back to the other. It was very supportive, and, in that sense, a positive contribution, because being a part-timer can be very difficult. Everyone was so committed that there was the problem of guilt. It was easy to doubt your commitment to the project because you were not always around or, perhaps, had to leave in the middle of a crisis to collect children. We needed the moral support of knowing that, between us, we covered a whole job. Even so, there were areas in which we did an awful lot less and this would have raised problems in the long run. The full-timers, for instance, tended inevitably to be the contact points.

In my present job we are all job-sharing, so it's a totally different ball-game. It sounds ideal. We share two jobs (divided into four) between three women, so we all work two-thirds time. Basically, we all work school hours and share the evening meetings, so it feels more like a job with flexibility than a part-time commitment. Even so, I feel deeply ambivalent about working less than full-time. Part of me feels that the situation is ideal because it enables me to do the work I'm committed to *and* have time with my children; the other part of me has strong impulses to work full-time. This has to do with the reality of how part-time work is seen by most employers, also with the family situation. When the wife works part-time it reinforces role-segregation. This has got worse with us. I am the one picking up the children, going to the school, and so on. And I think that my husband minds more than I do. He would like to contribute more equally.

The main value of job-sharing is getting part-time work on to the agenda, particularly in areas where it has not been available. But it's not the final answer, because it does not provide a living wage. For those women who are alone, or want to be financially independent of their partners, the pay is not enough.'

Jean and Mike. Community Workers

Jean and Mike have two children aged 6 and 3. For a time they job-shared for a small charitable trust company which has a commitment to shared child-care and shared work, but recently Jean has given up her part of the job and returned to the home.

Jean. 'The arrangement in our organisation is that you can take up to a year off after the birth of a child, and then you return to shared work. It does have the effects which it seeks to promote — you don't go cabbagy, or have an identity crisis — but it's not the perfect answer.

I was seven months pregnant with my first child when I started my job. My husband joined before me, and we lived on-site. My job evolved out of just being there, and I liked that. The needs of your children change and you may be able to do something one year which you are unable to do the next. To be in an organisation which can offer a variety of tasks, and tries to meet personal needs as this one does, is marvellous. I started off working on a city farm, and later worked specifically with under-fives.

Our jobs were separate, but together we put in one-and-a-half times full-time hours. Outside the times of meetings and a few specific arrangements, the hours you work can be flexible. The disadvantage was that we never saw each other, because while one of us was working the other was at home with the children. Our work spanned the evenings as well, because a full-time commitment entails 60 hours a week. Also, despite the lip-service paid to the principle of involving job-sharing parents, there was not an awful lot of understanding of their problems. Meetings, for instance, would be arranged for 5.30 pm.

I think our both working in that way had its good effects. It did challenge our sexist roles, and the children have grown up equally at home with both of us. Finally, however, I felt unable to solve the problem of commitment. As a part-time worker I felt that I was seen to be less committed and, in the end, the choice was between making more commitment, in the knowledge that the children would suffer, and full-time parenting at home. There were tensions in our marriage, and problems of personal growth. When was there time for *us*? However much you believe in the ethos of the group, if the demands upon you are too great what is the point? There is no glory in work for its own sake. So I resigned.'

Mike. 'We began the arrangement at my instigation, not Jean's. I was looking around for a place I wanted to work in and I came across this organisation. One of the things which attracted me was its consciousness of the needs of people. Pay is assessed on need, as opposed to there being a set salary. After necessary expenditure, the disposable income of everybody is meant to be the same.

We gave up a two-bedroomed house in Wimbledon and moved straight into squat accommodation on the city farm, so there was quite a lot of adjustment. We were certainly making a statement. The organisation is very conscious of the needs of women and I liked that. I was afraid, on Jean's behalf, of the bored, intelligent, competent person suffering from lack of access to creative involvement. I believed that if we job-shared she would be offered the maximum freedom to find work she enjoyed, on the basis of our sharing the care of the children.

The positive effects would have been more apparent if it had not been such a strain. I got a lot of satisfaction from knowing she was involved with work, and from the time I spent with the children, but it is difficult not to get too involved in the kind of work we were doing, and the way things turned out we were doing 90 hours a week between us. The children always had one of us, but not often both together, even at weekends. It fragmented the work, too. I can remember a day when I went into, and came away from, work six times to fit in with Jean's arrangements. I can't work that way.

It was not entirely the fault of the organisation. The workers have created a structure which, they hope, will cater for everyone's needs. For instance, there is even pay for parenting, for people who want to retain their commitment and return to active participation later. But, inevitably in any close group, differences of experience and views can create problems, and we found this was particularly the case with our group in which working and living are fairly inseparable. We could not entirely reconcile our family life with the group ethos and we needed a degree of separation which was difficult to achieve while we were both working.

Now that Jean has decided that her work is in the home, she has found a number of fulfilling interests and commitments and my job is much easier. I can concentrate and there is less disruption. It is better for our relationship, too, but I see less of the children and I regret that.'

Conclusion

Three main points seem to emerge. First, part-time employment is, for many women, a long-term arrangement to which, in comparison with full-timers, they make at least an equivalent commitment, and for which they receive less than equivalent rewards. Although less is known about male part-timers, it is clear that their opportunities are as limited, and their terms of employment as unfavourable, as those of women. In addition, they must contend with attitudes which effectively prevent them from having a free choice about whether they should work part-time. There is an urgent need for reform, so that part-timers receive equal protection under employment law, extended rights to occupational pensions, and negotiated benefits along the lines proposed in the motion passed at TUC Congress in 1986 (see Appendix A, p 177). The problem posed by the present inequitable situation affects not only the conditions of work during the period of part-timing, but also the total career prospects of those who do it. There is, therefore, a need for re-examination of the status of part-timers, and of the levels of responsibility they can assume, so that they do not suffer an undue setback in their career development. This could have a significant influence in improving the career performance of women.

Second, there are many women who sacrifice the benefits of employee status for the sake of convenience. Two measures could improve this situation: employee status should be extended as an automatic right to the most vulnerable group (the homeworkers and regular 'casual' workers) and a greater flexibility in working hours could be introduced to enable more people to take up permanent part-time positions. In this context, the introduction of statutory child-sickness leave, to be taken by either parent (as practised, for example in Scandinavian countries), would be helpful.

The third point is more complex. Organisations which have the welfare of workers at heart have tended to shun the issue of part-time work and to channel their disapproval of the inequities into campaigning for its removal. The unions discourage the employment of part-timers, though they may, to varying degrees, act on their behalf once they are employed. Feminists have been campaigning for day nurseries rather than dealing with the inequalities of part-time employment.

Many women, and some men, would prefer part-time hours, but are forced into full-time work for lack of viable alternatives. At the same time, people who do not wish it are currently being offered job-splits, and the numbers of unemployed are rising.

Research undertaken by the University of Warwick Institute of Employment Research in 1983 predicts unemployment levels above four million throughout the 1980s. At the same time, it suggests that the number of part-time employees could rise to five million plus by the early 1990s.

Another developing trend is towards the concept of the 'flexible firm', with a core of full-time workers who enjoy job security and high wages, supplemented by a large pool of temporary and part-time workers, and by self-employed sub-contractors and small firms. The advantages, from the *employer's* point of view, are clear: the workforce can easily be expanded or reduced in line with the demands of the business cycle. However, from the individual worker's point of view, the benefits of this trend are more doubtful. It *could* lead to a growth in the numbers of independent small businesses and self-employed freelance workers, able to operate flexibly and have a considerable degree of autonomy; on the other hand, it could mean that we move more and more towards a divided society, with expendable temporary and part-time workers, unrepresented by trade unions, who are wide open to exploitation.

The possibility of these developments makes it vital that part-timing is undertaken from *choice* and with full employment status and protection. Not only do we need reform along the lines already mentioned; we also need to reconsider our automatic acceptance of full-timing as the only viable form of work, and to create a flexible system within which part-time work can be extended. Part-timers, too, are workers, not merely 'hands'.

Part 3

Appendix A

Motion Passed at TUC Congress, 1986

'Congress notes that Britain's five million part-time workers suffer extensively and disproportionately from poverty pay, poor conditions of employment and inadequate rights at work.

Congress recognises that part-time workers should have equal status with those in full-time work, and that part-time work provides flexibility in working hours which is of great importance to men and women who care for children and dependent relatives.

Congress calls on the TUC to prepare a detailed report and policy statement on part-time workers which highlights the following issues:

(i)   the need to extend *employment rights* on matters such as unfair dismissal and maternity rights to part-time workers;

(ii) the need to extend rights to *occupational pensions*;

(iii) the need to ensure that *pay negotiations* take into account the special concerns and *conditions of employment* of part-time workers whose earnings often depend on basic wage rates and the hours they are able to work; and

(iv) the need to extend rights to contributory *social security benefits* and to remove the poverty trap faced by workers at the lower earnings limit for *National Insurance contributions*.

Congress calls on the TUC to use this statement to launch a better campaign for a better deal for part-timers and to press the Labour Party for action in this field by the next Labour Government.'

Appendix B

Lothian Health Board

Procedure for Two Doctors to Share a Whole-time Hospital Post (as from May 1975)

1. The Board has confirmed with the Scottish Home and Health Department that lack of a specific reference in the advertisement to the possibility of sharing the post between two doctors does not preclude consideration of such candidates.

2. Those who submit a joint application for a whole-time appointment are asked to agree that they will share all the duties of the post in a manner that is agreeable to them *and* acceptable to their future working colleagues. In addition, they are each asked if they also wish to be considered for the post on a whole-time basis.

3. Unless the post is to be shared on an unequal basis, contracts are offered to the successful candidates on a half-time basis and, if appropriate, the UMTs divided equally — with rounding up in the doctor's favour, if necessary.

4. If one of the 'twinned' doctors has to leave before the full term of her, or his, contract the following steps are taken:
   (a) the other 'half' of the post is offered to the remaining twin;
   (b) efforts are made to identify a new 'twin' to act as a locum until the end of the appointment;

   or failing either of these,
   (c) the Board advertise a vacancy in the usual way, recognising the remaining 'twin' as a supernumerary appointment until her, or his, contract comes to an end.

   As far as Terms and Conditions of Service are concerned these are applied to each of the doctors as individuals.

5. Both 'twins' are entitled to the normal annual/study leave and financial allowances but they are expected to take half their annual and study leave from their halves of the day/week in which they are not working, ie the leave allowances are x(½ weeks) and not ½(x weeks).

NB All vacant posts are scrutinised carefully before refilling especially in times when stringent cost limits are in force.

Appendix C

The Interviewees

Family Composition

All but one of the interviewees were women and all but one had at least one child below the age of 16. The majority had children in the primary age range, and smaller proportions had pre-school and teenage children. There were five single parents, of whom three were totally dependent on their part-time earnings to support themselves and their families. Of the rest, all but three considered their earnings a necessary contribution to the family income.

Men are under-represented in the survey. In line with statistics nationally, a sample of 32 part-timers should include five men. This imbalance can be attributed to the author's method of finding respondents, which was largely through a network of one person leading to another, as long as a reasonably representative spread of occupations was achieved. Had men emerged through this procedure, they would have been included. As it was, they remained a hidden factor.

Employment Status

Of the 32 people interviewed, 21 were employees and 11 had more insecure forms of employment as homeworkers (1), casual workers (1) and freelancers or self-employed people (9). Of the non-employees, only three were continuing part-time with their full-time mode of work. The rest had accepted the conditions in response to their domestic situation. Four of the employees were job-sharers (all in professional posts) and there was one job-sharer who was freelancing because this was the only basis on which her employer would accept the arrangement. Of the people with employee status, four worked for less than 16 hours a week and therefore had no job security. No employee worked for less than eight hours weekly.

Earnings

The interviews were conducted between October 1982 and April 1983 and at this time there was a high proportion (7) of people earning less than £29.50 a week (the then current National Insurance contributions threshold) and though two of these were self-employed people working only a few hours a week, one was a domestic worker who worked for 20 hours. Apart from this, earnings were fairly evenly spread.

Five people earned between £29.50 and £50 weekly, four working between 20 and 25 hours in a variety of non-professional occupations and one working for fewer hours on average as a professional freelancer.

Eight earned between £50 and £70 weekly, again in a variety of occupations. A feature of this group was the increased number of hours worked to earn this money. Although all considered themselves to be part-timers, one worked for 33 hours, one for between 30 and 40, one for 40 hours, and one worked in excess of 50 hours a week.

The largest group earned more than £70 weekly, but less than £6,000 annually. Six of these were in professional occupations, two working for fewer than 16 hours a week. Of the remaining four, two were skilled office workers working around 25 hours.

Two interviewees earned more than £6,000 annually. Both had demanding jobs and worked long hours (in terms of part-time work) to earn their salaries.

Reasons for Giving Up Full-time Employment

Pregnancy was the most frequent reason cited (19), with a scattering of others connected with the domestic situation as follows: marriage (2); children reaching school age and leaving all-day nurseries (2); moving home for husband's job (3); domestic crisis (1) and illness (1). One interviewee had never worked full-time. Only three people gave personal development or preference as the reason for leaving full-time employment. All the others had, to some extent, been the victims of circumstance.

Status and Promotion Prospects

Four people had taken a straightforward drop in status in their previous occupation and three had moved to lower status jobs. Of the others, the status of the professional freelancers is difficult to define or equate with their previous full-time employment, though one was quite definite about the dull nature of the assignments she was offered. The vast majority of the remainder had been in fairly humble jobs to begin with and there was little subsequent change. Several, however, had found part-time jobs which were more demanding and rewarding than their previous full-time employment.

Taking the people with employee status as a group (21), 11 were not eligible for promotion as part-timers, against five who were. The issue did not arise for a further five, three of them because they worked in establishments with a non-hierarchical staffing structure, and two of them because they worked in small units where higher grades of employment did not exist.

Employer-initiated Training

Taking the employees as the group for whom this matter is relevant, 14 had received no such training, though one of this number expected, later, to take advantage of the training facilities available. Of the remaining seven, one had access to professional support sessions, one was occupying a medical training post, two had attended training courses and the remaining three had received on-the-job training.

Terms and Conditions of Employment

The self-employed group (11) had no employment benefits. Of the employees (21), all but one received paid holidays. Seventeen received the same rate of pay as equivalent full-timers and one considered that she received more. Three were in jobs for which there were no full-time equivalents. This apparently satisfactory situation does not take account of the possible loss of earnings through workers being confined to low grades of employment, low-status jobs and through ineligibility to overtime or unsocial hours payments.

Seven were eligible for inclusion in a company or professional pension scheme (all but two of them in professional occupations), and 14 were not.

Pressure of Work

Of the total group, 12 considered that they worked under more pressure than full-timers, and 12 considered that they did not. Of the remaining eight, one sometimes felt under more pressure, three had no equivalent full-timers with whom to compare themselves and four freelancers felt that the question did not apply to them. Pressure was felt by people in professional occupations (5), by the self-employed (4) and by office workers (3).

Working Hours

Leaving aside the people who worked at home, and therefore selected their own working hours, 24 people worked at a workplace, including three who were self-employed. Of these, 10 worked a shortened day, three worked mornings only and two worked evenings only. The remaining eight worked a combination of hours involving a mixture of full and half days, of half days and evenings, and one regular early morning shift. Four had some flexibility to arrange their hours, but also needed to do some evening work.

Two people had arrangements which enabled them to take the school holidays off work, and two more, by the nature of their jobs, were on holiday at these times. With the exception of the doctor, no one worked nights. Nevertheless, nine people were, to some extent, working unsocial hours.

The Employers

Ten employees worked in the public sector, five of them in domestic jobs, four in professional posts and one as an office worker. Of the 11 employees in the private sector, only one worked for a large company, and three worked in establishments employing fewer than six workers.

Union Membership

Within the total group, about a third of the interviewees (11) were members of a trade union. Of these, seven were employed in the public sector, two were non-employees, one worked for a voluntary group and one for a firm operating a closed shop. The non-members were predominantly people working for small private employers (9) and the self-employed (9). Only three public sector employees did not belong to a union.

Length of Employment

Taking the length of employment of the non-employees to mean the length of time during which each person had engaged in the same type of work part-time on a non-employee basis, and the length of employment of the employees as the period of employment part-time with the same employer, the picture is one of stability. The largest group (9) had been in the same employment for between five and 10 years. Seven people had remained in the same employment for more than 10 years and a further eight for between one and three years. Four people had a record of between three and five years, and four (a mere 12½ per cent) had been in their jobs for less than a year. There were no marked differences between occupational groups. Those who had been longest in their jobs comprised two domestic and one catering worker, one shop worker and three professionals, and those who had been in their jobs for under a year were one domestic worker, two office workers and one shop worker. The only 'bunching' was in the one- to three-year group, where five of the eight workers were people in professional occupations. Perhaps the wish for career development caused these people to move on after a certain length of time. Constant and unconstructive changes between employers and occupations was not a feature of the group as a whole.

Appendix D

The Role of Jobcentres

Jobcentres are to be found in any High Street. They are run by the Employment Services Division of the Manpower Services Commission and their function is two-fold. They are the Government's job-finding agencies, carrying a variety of job advertisements on their boards, and they act as agencies for the Government-sponsored re-training scheme known as the Job Training Scheme (see below).

In the past, all people who registered as unemployed were automatically registered with their local Jobcentre, but this practice has now been discontinued. You can use your Jobcentre in one of two ways. You can go in and browse among the job advertisements and seek an introduction for any likely job without further obligation or commitment, or you can become registered with the Jobcentre. If you take the latter course, you will be asked for details of your qualifications and experience, and of the kind of job you are looking for, and you will then be informed when any suitable vacancies arise. It is clearly advisable to become registered if you are seriously seeking work.

Jobcentres are easy to use. Part-time posts are advertised on separate boards, often under occupational headings, and there are clear instructions about how you should use the services provided. The Jobcentre makes the initial contact with a potential employer on your behalf, whether you are registered or not, and subsequently arranges your interview with the employer if he or she agrees to see you.

As Jobcentres are run by the Government, all rulings of the Race Relations and Sex Discrimination Acts which bear upon recruitment of employees should be strictly observed. However, it is important to note that it is the employer, not the Jobcentre, who selects the employee.

Courses

Manpower Services Commission Adult Training Programmes

These are training courses run by the Training Services division of the Manpower Services Commission, and are geared towards re-training or updating skills in a wide variety of areas.

The Job Training Scheme

This scheme replaces the old TOPS (Training Opportunities) scheme.

It offers a wide choice of training, to equip people with better skills in a wide variety of fields — from craft skills and office work to computing, technician, technologist and management occupations. The scheme includes opportunities for basic skills training for people who wish to work in the automotive, construction, electronics, and mechanical engineering industries, and in retailing and commerce. There are also opportunities for skilled people who wish to learn about new techniques in their trade or who wish to improve and update the skills they already have.

You can apply for most courses if you:

— are unemployed and at least 18 years old
— have been away from full-time education for at least two years
— intend to look for a job which uses your new skills
— normally live and are allowed to work in Great Britain.

Courses generally last from three to six months, though some last for up to one year. Most courses are full-time, and you normally receive a training allowance to live on while you are on the course. There are also some part-time courses, where you will not receive an allowance, but your travelling expenses will be paid.

Wider Opportunities Training

If you have been unemployed for a while and would like to make a fresh start, but are not sure which direction to take, you may find a 'Wider Opportunities' training course helpful.

Wider Opportunities Training comes in different forms and courses may have different names. They offer both flexible timing (eg three days a fortnight) and flexible training, designed to help you find a job locally, with local conditions in mind. The courses last anything from a few days to several weeks.

Training for Enterprise

It is worth noting, too, that the MSC run a range of courses for people thinking of setting up their own businesses, including a self-employment programme for those who plan a small-scale one-women (or one-man) business.

If you are interested in the Job Training Scheme, Wider Opportunities Training or Training for Enterprise, call in at your local Jobcentre or ring the nearest Manpower Services Commission Training Division Area Office.

Other Courses

For courses leading specifically to re-entry to a known occupation, see the appropriate chapters, and the list of addresses on pp 186-187.

If you would like to enter higher education, but lack the academic requirements for entry, you may be accepted on an Access course. These were started in 1978 to bring intending students up to the required educational level and to provide a structure within which they could increase their confidence to tackle more demanding forms of education. Most courses are held at further education colleges which maintain links with appropriate institutions of higher education. For further details, inquire at your local polytechnic or college of further education or consult the directory of Access courses produced by the University of Lancaster School of Education (see Bibliography).

A number of other courses, many of them part-time, have been started with the aim of opening up opportunities for people who might otherwise feel limited in the choice available to them. Newcastle University, for instance, runs a New Opportunities for Women (NOW) course, one day a week for two terms. For further details, inquire at any local institutions of higher education.

Evening Institute classes, run under the auspices of local education authorities, also provide the means of broadening your horizons. If you cannot find a particular subject which interests you, you may benefit from taking a general orientation course for women if one is available in your area. Women's studies is also an expanding field. Your local library will have a handbook listing all evening institute classes. Tuition fees are nominal.

For information about Pre-School Playgroups courses, contact the national headquarters: Pre-School Playgroups Association, Alford House, Aveline Street, London SE11 5DH.

Bibliography

Armstrong, J (1982) 'Leicester Outwork Campaign – action research with the hidden army'. Leicester Community Work Training Unit.

Beaumont, B (1979) 'Special provisions for women doctors to train and practise in medicine after graduation: a report of a survey'. *Medical Education*, 13, 4, 284-91. July

Boyle, A (1980) 'Job-sharing. A study of the costs, benefits and employment rights of job-sharers'. New Ways to Work and the Equal Opportunities Commission.

Chaney, J (1981) 'Social networks and job information: the situation of women who return to work'. Equal Opportunities Commission/Social Services Research Council.

Crine, S (1979) 'The hidden army'. Low Pay Unit.

Darling, M (1975) *The Role of Women in the Economy*. Organisation for Economic Co-operation and Development, Paris.

Day, P (1982) *Women Doctors. Choices and Constraints in Policies for Medical Manpower*. King's Fund Centre.

Department of Health and Social Security (1981) 'Remember how it felt to be a nurse?'

Elias, P and Main, B (1982) 'Women's working lives. Evidence from the National Training Survey'. University of Warwick, Institute for Employment Research.

Equal Opportunities Commission (1976) 'Equal Pay. A guide to the Equal Pay Act 1970'.

Equal Opportunities Commission (1977) 'Equal Pay for women – what you should know about it'.

Equal Opportunities Commission (1978) 'I want to work, but what about the kids? Day care for your children and opportunities for working parents'.

Equal Opportunities Commission (1979) 'How to prepare your own case for an Industrial Tribunal'.

Equal Opportunities Commission (1981) 'Job-sharing. Improving the quality and availability of part-time work'.

Equal Opportunities Commission (1982) 'Equality at work. A guide to the employment provisions of the Sex Discrimination Act 1975'.

Department of Employment (1981) 'Statutory minimum wages and holidays with pay'. The Wages councils Act briefly explained.

Federation of Personal Services of Great Britain (1975) 'The temporary. A national survey of attitudes, comments and regional statistics'.

General and Municipal Workers Union (1981) 'Equality at work. The way forward'. A GMWU guide for negotiators.

Gilbert, S and Mason, A (1980) 'The Employment Act 1980 and why we must fight it'. Rights of Women

Haringey Women's Employment Project (undated) 'Why aren't we counted? Women's unemployment and the return to work'.

Haringey Women's Employment Project/Lewisham Women and Employment Project (undated) 'Women: where are your jobs going?' A study of women's unemployment in Haringey and Lewisham.

Hurstfield, J (1978) 'The part-time trap: part-time workers in Britain today'. Low Pay Unit.

Huws, Ursula (1984) *The New Homeworkers.* Low Pay Unit.

Lewis, D (1983) *Essentials of Employment Law.* Institute of Personnel Management.

Lindley, R M and Whitley, J D (eds) (1983) *Review of the Economy and Employment.* Institute for Employment Research, University of Warwick.

Lucas S and Ward, P (1985) 'A Survey of "Access" Courses in England'. University of Lancaster School of Education.

MacLennon, E (1980) 'Minimum wages for women'. An examination of women's earnings in industries covered by wages councils. Low Pay Unit and EOC.

MSC Training Services Division (1981) 'No barriers here'. A guide to career development issues in the employment of women.

Maric, D (1975) *Adapting Working Hours to Modern Needs.* International Labour Office, Geneva.

Moss, P and Fonda, N (1980) *Work and the Family.* Temple Smith.

National Joint Committee of Working Women's Organisations (undated) 'Women's right to work'.

New Ways to Work (1982) 'Job-sharing: a guide for employees'.

Rees, T and Read, M (1981) 'Equality?' Report of a survey of NALGO members. National and Local Government Officers' Association.

Reid, E (1976) 'Women workers in society'. *International Perspectives.* International Labour Office, Geneva.

Robarts, S, Coote, A and Ball, E (1981) 'Positive action for women. The next step'. National Council for Civil Liberties, Rights for Women Unit.

Robinson, O (1979) 'Part-time employment in the European Community'. *International Labour Review*, May-June.

Sedley, A (1980) 'Part-time workers need full-time rights'. National Council for Civil Liberties, Rights for Women Unit.

Select Committee on the European Communities (1982) *Voluntary Part-time Work.* Minutes of submissions to Committee in respect of the proposed EEC Directive on Part-time Work. HMSO.

Trades Union Council (1983) 'Women in the labour market'.

Welsh Women's Aid (1982) 'Available for work?' A study of the Rayner Test of availability for work in Cardiff, Ebbw Vale and Leeds.

Useful Addresses

General

Equal Opportunities Commission
Overseas House
Quay Street
Manchester M3 3HN

Low Pay Unit
9 Upper Berkeley Street
London W1H 8BY

Manpower Services Commission
Moorfoot
Sheffield S1 4PQ

National Council for Civil Liberties
21 Tabard Street
London SE1 4LA

Ante-Natal Teaching

The National Childbirth Trust
9 Queensborough Terrace
London W2 3TB

Homeworking

Leicester Outwork Campaign
132 Regent's Road
Leicester
(There are also homeworking
projects in the London Boroughs of
Camden, Greenwich, Hackney,
Haringey, Islington, Lambeth and
Southwark. Contact the local
council for further details.)

Job-sharing

New Ways to Work
309 Upper Street
London N1 2TY
(Job-sharing register)

Hackney Job-Share Project
Shoreditch Town Hall
Old Street
London EC1V 9LT
(have undertaken special studies of
job-sharing for teachers)

Sheffield Job-sharing Group
c/o Ann Wood
Sheffield Careers and
    Appointments Service
AUEW House
Furnival Gate
Sheffield S1 3HE

Law

The Law Society
113 Chancery Lane
London WC2A 1PL

The Inns of Court School of Law
4 Gray's Inn Place
London WC1R 5DX

Legal advice for women

Rights of Women
52 Featherstone Street,
London EC1Y 8RT

Medicine

The Medical Women's Federation
Tavistock House North
Tavistock Square
London WC1H 9HX

The Council for Postgraduate
    Medical Education
7 Marylebone Road
London NW1 5HH

Nursing

English National Board
Careers Advisory Centre
26 Margaret Street
London W1N 7LR

Welsh Office
Nursing Division
Crown Offices
Cathays Park
Cardiff CF1 3NQ

National Board for Northern
Ireland
RAC House
79 Chichester Street
Belfast BT1 4JR

MET Division
Scottish Health Service Centre
Crewe Road South
Edinburgh EH4 2LF
(for initial training inquiries)

Scottish National Board
22 Queen Street
Edinburgh EH2 1JX
(for post-initial training inquiries)

Office work

Part Time Careers Ltd
10 Golden Square
London W1R 3AF

Professional associations

CHIROPODY
Society of Chiropodists
53 Welbeck Street
London W1M 7HE

DISPENSING AND
    OPHTHALMIC OPTICS
General Optic Council
41 Harley Street
London W1N 2DJ

INDEXING
The Society of Indexers
123a Queens Crescent
London NW5 4HE

also
Rapid Results College
Tuition House
London SW19 4DS

OCCUPATIONAL THERAPY
College of Occupational Therapists
20 Rede Place
London W2 4TU

ORTHOPTICS
British Orthoptic Society
Tavistock House North
Tavistock Square
London WC1H 9HX

PHYSIOTHERAPY
Chartered Society of Physiotherapy
14 Bedford Row
London WC1R 4ED

RADIOGRAPHY
College of Radiographers
14 Upper Wimpole Street
London W1M 8BN

SPEECH THERAPY
College of Speech Therapists
Harold Poster House
6 Lechmere Road
London NW2 5BU

TRANSLATION
The Translators' Guild
24a Highbury Grove
London N5 2EA

also
Translators Association
Society of Authors
84 Drayton Gardens
London SW10 9SD

Wages Council

Wages Inspectorate
Department of Employment
Hanway House
27 Red Lion Square
London WC1R 4NH
also

Office of Wages Councils
Steel House
11 Tothill Street
London SW1H 9YY

Women's Employment

Welsh Women's Aid
33 Adam Street
Cardiff CF1 2TY

Index

ACAS (Advisory Conciliation and Arbitration Service), 29
'Access' courses, 89, 183
Acts of Parliament, 27-40
Additional Pension, 50-51
Advisory Conciliation and Arbitration Service (ACAS), 29
agencies, employment, 54, 85-6
  domestic cleaning, 97
Agricultural Wages Board, 128
agriculture:
  employment statistics, 23, 128
  pay, 128
  work in, 128-9
alternate weeks, working, 57-8
ante-natal teaching, case studies in, 153-5
appeals procedures, 31-3
attitudes to work, part-timers', 84-5

Banking, 57-8
Barclays' Bank, 57
barristers, 161-2
BBC, case study in job-sharing at, 136-7

Camden Council, job-sharing policies of, 59
career break, returning to work following a, 79-80
career patterns, 85-6
catering, 100-107
childcare facilities, availability of, 72-6
childminders, facilities provided by, 74
cleaning work, 91-100
Community Law Centres, work in, 161
community medicine, 149-50
community nursing, 140, 142-3
Community Programme, 69
community work, 166
  case studies, 170-72
company pension schemes, 51-2
'continuous employment', legislation and, 34-6
contract of employment, 26, 43-4
Council for Postgraduate Medical Education, 146

Council for Professions Supplementary to Medicine, 143
courses, training, 182-3

Day nurseries, availability of, 73
dentistry, 150-51
  case studies, 152-3, 157
Dentists' Retainer Scheme, 150
DHSS (Department of Health and Social Security), 25
DHSS Circular (PM[79]3), 147, 150
disabled people, 27-8
Disabled Persons Employment Act 1944, 27-8
discrimination:
  racial, 28, 30
  sex, 28-30, 31-2
dismissal, unfair, 36-7, 39-40
doctors, 144-50
  case study, 155-6
domestic work, 91-100

Earnings *see* pay
education, female workers', 14-16
  see also training
elderly people, facilities for care of, 76
electrical manufacturing, 123-4
Elias, Peter, 17, 20-21, 70, 77
employee, legal definition of, 26
employment, contract of, 26, 43-4
Employment Act 1980, 29, 33, 37, 39
Employment Act 1982, 33, 37
employment agencies *see* agencies
Employment Appeals Tribunal, 32
Employment Gazette, 17
Employment Protection Act 1975, 33
Employment Protection (Consolidation) Act 1978, 26
employment rights, 25-44
employment statistics, 14, 16-17, 174
  see also under individual industries, eg agriculture
English National Board Careers Advisory Centre, 140
Equal Pay Act 1970, 29, 30, 32-3
'equal value' concept, 32
Equality for Women within Trade Unions (TUC Charter), 41